Paraffin Lights – Water from the Well

A rural ride of growing up in Sussex – before, during and after World War II

Paraffin Lights –
Water from the Well

A rural ride of growing up in Sussex –
before, during and after World War II

By
Michael G. Butcher
assisted by
Sussex Author
David J. Knowles

Published by
Knowles Publishing
Rochester

First published 2000
Knowles Publishing. Rochester

ISBN 09534358 3 0

Front cover photograph:

Fletching Mill

Back Cover

(Print of Painting)
'Wings Over Chailey'

By Barry Weekley

Published by Knowles Publishing. Rochester

Typeset by Academic & Technical Typesetting, Bristol
Printed by Redwood Books, Trowbridge, Wilts.

Dedication

This book is dedicated to my wife Rosemary and the rest of the family, for having faith in me to finish what I started.

Acknowledgments

My thanks to:

Bill Howe, for allowing me to use some words from his book 'Fletching' and also an account about the Canadians from the booklet 'Festival of Fletching' – and also for the photographs.

John Pye and Henry Robinson for information about farming at that time. Barry Dickens for various photographs. Michael S. Welch author of Rails to Sheffield Park, for photographs. Klaus Marks – archivist of The Bluebell Railway, for photographs and information. Hendon R.A.F Museum for information about Chailey Airfield. Jack and Gwen Soames and Fred and Ada Gladman, for information about pre war Fletching.

East Sussex Records Office for their help and, particularly, for information taken from the Sussex Constabulary Archive, about P.C. Cuthbert Meads – the village policeman at Fletching for thirty one years.

Brighton Referance Library and Newhaven Library for all their patience.

Brighton Evening Argus, The Sussex Express and County Herald, Kent and Sussex Courier, The Times. Imperial War Museum.

Spitfire Art and artist Barry Weekley for his painting – 'Wings Over Chailey' (see back cover).

Ron Farrant for help with transport. Peter Simmons for E. Mail help. Ellie and Maggie, my tutors on the enjoyable Creative Writing Course at Newhaven and my fellow students for encouraging and supporting me in this project. My Wife Rosemary for the numerous cups of tea.

Sussex author David J. Knowles for helping me to put the book together and for all the ghostwriting and editing. Also his wife Pamela for all the computer work she has done and anyone else, not mentioned here, who has helped in any way to get this book to be – more than just a dream.

Contents

Illustrations

Paraffin Lights –
Water From The Well

Foreword
By Sussex Author
David J. Knowles

L ike many others who are avid readers particularly of books that tell of times gone by, of local history and the ways of life in the working and leisure times of our forefathers – I find, with great regret, that so little has been written by those who actually lived in the villages and hamlets of rural England through centuries gone by, and even of such a small span of time as – 'just a hundred years or so ago.'

In my writings over the last few years, I have written a book about a childhood in Brighton during the traumatic years of the second world war, and another one about a particular year shortly after the turmoil of that – "war to end all wars" – and, at the end of those books, in the authors 'bits,' I have said that I would be delighted to help anyone who wants to write of his or her lives – during the nineteen thirties and forties in particular – and I hope that, at least, this period of time will be well recorded for those of future generations with 'like minds' to myself.

In response to my offer, I received a letter from a gentleman who was brought up in a Sussex village – his formative years including the ones I have mentioned. The village that Michael Butcher was brought up in is called Fletching; it is one of several villages that are situated near the banks of the river Ouse in Sussex.

I was very pleased to agree to help Michael with his writings, not only because of the particular time span, but also because the Sussex Ouse played a large part in the early years of my own life and I can recall many adventures on and around its waters – times etched forever, nostalgically, in my mind.

Some say that the Sussex Ouse starts as a trickle at St. Leonards Forest, near Horsham, others will say that it begins its life at Balcombe and eventually joins the trickle from St. Leonards Forest at Slaugham – not many miles away. Wherever the source is – the river remains young as it runs by Fletching and matures when it gets to Isfield on its way to Lewes, before eventually reaching the sea at Newhaven.

The rivers and villages of Sussex are steeped in the history of England, in its farming and industry over the centuries – even the politics and wars of those distant days.

Michael's writings, although of times not all that long ago, are none the less of an age, the likes of which – unfortunately in many ways – we will never see again. Also, those years include the dark, sometimes sad, yet vivid and 'uniting' days of World War II. During those years of austerity and danger, the people of the United Kingdom were brought together in an unforgettable way – 'we were all in the same boat together.'

In Fletching, during the years when Michael was growing up, he was to witness much upheaval and see many new faces suddenly appear on the scene – including the Canadian soldiers, who were billeted all around the village and in many other nearby places, during the bitter conflict of World War II. It was a time for new adventures and, also, a time when precautions, such as carrying gas masks everywhere and seeking shelter the moment the siren ominously sounded, were the order of the day.

After the war it soon became noticeable to Michael that the pre-war ways of life were fast disappearing but, in going through his manuscript, I was delighted to read of happenings of that not too distant time ago which included traditional ways of life that go back through the centuries.

So without further words from me, I will leave it to the reader to enjoy an account of life in rural Sussex, through a span of years which, for the many who lived through them, are quite simply – unforgettable, unforgotten.

Chapter One

Early History – A River of Character

By the time the sirens blared out on that warm Sunday morning in 1939, I had already celebrated eight birthdays in the village that was to become so much a part of my life during the formative years of growing up. The war was to bring about many changes in our ways of life and we were soon to witness extraordinary happenings as England prepared for the worst that might come in the weeks, months – even years ahead.

The village I was born in, on a breezy, coolish day in May 1931, is called Fletching. As the crow flies it is about nine miles in a northerly direction from Lewes, the county town of East Sussex, and just over two miles from the small town of Uckfield. In telling something of Fletching's origins, I think that a small book called 'Fletching' by Bill Howe – a local resident and one time chairman of the parish council – is probably the most apt in its descriptions of 'through the ages' to quote from here and I do so with Bill's permission.

'The origins of Fletching as a place of human habitation are lost in antiquity, but the 'ing' termination of it's name, almost certainly proves that it was one of the very early settlements of the Anglo-Saxons, who invaded this country during the latter part of the fifth century and established themselves on or near the banks of navigable rivers. The 'ing' termination means 'the people of,' and there can be little doubt that Fletching owes its name to some tribal chieftain of the invaders called 'Flecci' or something very like it. The alternative theory that the name derives from the French word 'Fleche,' which means 'Arrow,' does not hold water, for the Domesday record shows that the name was well established long before the village became known for its manufacture of arrow heads, some of them used in the battles of Crecy and Poitiers – in 1346 and 1356.

Both Fletching and Sheffield Park, which is in the parish, are enumerated in the Domesday Book where they are referred to as 'Flescinge and Siffelle.'

In the early days of my life I was taken on walks around the area by my parents and many of the landmarks soon became familiar sights to me. One of the places we used to go by was Clinton Lodge, which was situated at the end of the High Street. This was a small Georgian style house, with outbuildings and a large formal garden. Locals used to say that when you take in the magnificent and uninterrupted view of the South Downs from these gardens '– if you can see the Downs clearly, it's going to rain; if you can't see them – it's already raining!'

The gardens used to be the venue for the village fete before the war and was owned by Mr. And Mrs. Hardinge –

14

who opened the gardens to the public in summer time. There was a flower show held during the afternoon and also, childrens sports as well as music supplied by the Uckfield Town Band.

My own first memories of the geography of the countryside, just beyond the safe and familiar confines of home and in the village, are of mysterious and exciting areas of woodlands, fields, lakes, streams and rivers, which looked to be ideal places for discovering and spending as much time as possible in – whilst creating all sorts of imaginative and explorative adventures.

However, before telling of growing up in such surroundings, I feel some more should be told of Fletching's history and some words that come to mind that I feel would also be very apt at the beginning of this book, can be found in James Turle's – 'The England I Love Best.' In his beautiful and informative book he describes the river Ouse, which runs just by Fletching on its way to Lewes before eventually entering the sea at Newhaven. He says:

'If a man would know what Sussex is, and something of what Sussex was, let him not waste his time beside the sea, let him not spend his days upon the Downs alone, nor hide himself with the wooded weald, nor follow the Sussex roads from one town into another, be it from east or from west. Let him rather walk afoot the banks of a Sussex river, starting above the weald, and making his way downwards and southwards towards the sea.' He goes on to say, '– and of all the Sussex rivers, I think the Ouse is the one that leads

15

you first into the heart of Sussex. For the Sussex Ouse is a kind river, a river that will take you to her heart and teach you to love her, and she will leave with you a little of that spirit of the Ouse which once given can never be wholly lost.'

Of the local history over the centuries, Turle tells of Simon DeMontford and the battle of Lewes:

'On the evening of May the thirteenth 1264, Simon DeMontford was marching on Lewes where King Henry the third's army was waiting for a night before continuing on its way to attack the Cinque Ports. On the fourteenth, the kings army was hurriedly drawn up in front of the town, with the Ouse and the marshes behind. The rebels came down in the morning over the downs from the west, and took the kings army by surprise; the royalists were cut off from retreats by the Ouse and Simon's victory was complete.

In the winter of 1348, the villages and rural communities of the Ouse valley, like so many other areas throughout the country, were devastated by the arrival of the Black Death. The disease killed off so many that, when it was over, the population had been decimated to the extent that employers had to double the wages of those working on the fields in order to get the work done. Also, many of the old wooden houses were burnt, because it was felt that the disease might linger here.

In olden times the Sussex Ouse was a busy river, navigated from as far as Lindfield and one can still see the remains of locks, used in the days when iron was smelted from various Sussex furnaces, including the one at Sheffield Park.

16

There are still plenty of connections to be found of olden days trading in foreign countries and many old ships timbers can still be found on farms near to the river – timber that found such usages as props, stays or even foot bridges over small tributaries. These timbers were brought up the river from Newhaven and then carted on carriages, so that perhaps, after hazardous sea voyages, the old oak wood returned to its Sussex home – even to the very farm or parish from where it first went.

Although there was plenty of trading done at the port of Newhaven; Lewes was also a busy trading centre on the river, with ships of up to thirty tons sometimes arriving under sail from various ports around the world. Their cargoes were usually of an assortment of pots, pans and anvils, or cannon and shot, carried under special licence, which would be unloaded – eventually to be taken on to London or the west country. Later, in the 17th century, fish, prunes, spices, hops, vinegar, salt and textiles, including paper and glass were also imported, and when the river was canalised, Lewes became the distributive point for upstream and downstream traffic.

Of the origins of the iron industry in Sussex, it is believed that this first started in medieval times, when there was a marked increase in the industry in England. One of the effects of the iron industry in Sussex was to denude the forests – although the timber for ships had almost as great an effect. This is when the canals came into good usage, but it is unlikely that the upper Ouse canal could have been commercially viable. Apart from Lewes, it served only small towns and villages such as – Fletching, Lindfield and Newick. Towpaths were constructed and wharves built beside the river near these villages. Records show that in 1801 Lewes was the base for 27 barges, but only seven of these operated upstream. There were two based at Barcombe and one at Hamsey, but a mere 10 horse drawn barges reflected only a small trade. New industries were optimistically created. Four paper mills functioned along the upper Ouse in the first half of the nineteenth century, but all were in decline by mid century. Inns were set up to cater for the bargees and they were suitably named – 'The Anchor' at Barcombe, 'The Sloop' at Freshfield and the 'The Horse and Barge' at Piltdown, and the first two of these still stand beside the river today – but serve a very different type of traveller to those who took refreshment in them in those hard working and colourful days.

The Ouse canal transported chalk and other materials for railway embankments, as well as flints, stone, timber and other requirements for track construction. However, transporting this material for the construction of the railway sounded the death knell for the Ouse to be navigable north of Hamsey, because, of course, the railway was cheaper and quicker, and quite soon the locks became weed covered and vegetation grew along the tow paths.

Other industries associated with the Ouse were the water mills, of which there were a great many – most of them grist mills. In other words for grain, but of course – 'grist for the mill' – means anything that can be turned into a profit, so sometimes the mills took advantage of other avenues of work as well.

Although there are no barges that ply their trade on the river now, the fields that lay by the river banks haven't changed too much and there are still many stretches where the walker can find something of the old serenity. I still find good tranquillity when walking along stretches of the banks of the Ouse near to Fletching – places very familiar to me in my youth – and, in doing so, I sometimes recall to my mind what Isaac Walton once said: "Rivers and the inhabitants of the watery element were made for wise men to contemplate and fools to pass by without consideration."

Most of the mills near to the Ouse have now disappeared, and none of them still operate today, but during those busy times, particularly at the end of the nineteenth century, there were mills at such places as – Slaugham, Fletching, Isfield, Barcombe, Uckfield, Sheffield, Shortbridge, Freshfield, Haywards Heath, Cockhaise and Lindfield.

Concerning Fletching, there are just a few more bits of local history, going back to earlier times, that I would like to mention here.

It is said that on the eve of the Battle of Lewes, Simon DeMontford with some Barons and other dignitaries, came to the church of St. Andrew and St. Mary the Virgin at Fletching, to pray for victory the following day – and there is a legend that a number of Simon's knights, who were slain in the battle with Henry The Third's army, were brought back and buried in full armour beneath the nave of the church.

Another famous name connected with Fletching is that of historian Edward Gibbon – author of 'The Decline and Fall of the Roman Empire.' He was a great friend of the first Earl Of Sheffield – John Baker Holroyd.

Gibbon actually wrote 'Decline and Fall' at Sheffield Park – this was during the years 1776 – 1778, and after spending the last few months of his life there he was buried, on his death in 1794, in the Sheffield family mausoleum which is in the north transit of the church.

The manor of Sheffield was bought in the late 18th century by John Baker Holroyd who commissioned James Wyatt to build him a new mansion in fashionable Gothic/ revival style. The extensive gardens at Sheffield Park were also laid out at this time, and include a series of woodlands and lakes that cover an area of some one hundred acres. These are now owned by the National Trust, and are open to the public between certain hours for most of the year. The colours are a sight to behold in the changing seasons – especially, of course, in spring and autumn and these extensive gardens were laid out by the famous Lancelot 'Capability' Brown.

The property remained in the Sheffield family until the death of the Third Earl on 1909; he was the person who was first responsible for the Australians to send a cricket team to tour this country. The first match of that tour was played on the magnificent ground in Sheffield Park – now no longer there, unfortunately. To play the Australians, Lord Sheffield would get together a team which would be as good as the one that represented England – with players of the calibre of W.G. Grace. The last game to be played against the Australians here was in 1896, but the name Sheffield lives on in cricket in Australia, as the inter-state matches are played for 'The Sheffield Shield' – a piece of silverware presented by the first earl.

So much, briefly, of some of the local history of times long gone. By the 1930's, the march of time was increasing in momentum and, although in my earliest years I was unaware of much or anything of the history of where I lived, I was, none the less, born at a time that would soon see major changes and become something of a far cry from what had been the popularly acceptable ways of living and patterns for life, handed down through countless generations.

Chapter Two

Paraffin Lights – Water From The Well

In 1931, the year of my birth, quite a lot of areas in the country were suffering the effects of the depression and there were high unemployment figures in many of the industrial areas. In the mid thirties the Jarrow march highlighted this depressing time, which was best described by one eminent politician as – "a national shame" – and the march soon got the attention it deserved. However, the unemployment was by no means endemic and the farming areas, in counties such as Sussex, remained mostly untouched by the breakdown in many industries – and so, employment on the land was mainly unaffected

The news more locally, during the week I was born, was centred on Princess Mary's visit to open The New Sussex Hospital in Windlesham Road in Brighton – the papers reported that there were huge crowds to watch this special visit.

For my parents, life after my birth carried on very much as beforehand, except that for the first few months of my life they hired a nursemaid for me. This was fairly unusual, for they were ordinary working class people and must have found it difficult to raise the wherewithal.

We lived in one of a pair of adjoining, weather- boarded, slate roofed houses on the outskirts of Fletching village. At that time we had no electricity or running water; the water had to be drawn from a well, which was just in front of the house in the small front garden. The water was drawn up by the means of a windlass, but one of the draw backs to this system of obtaining water was losing the bucket off the end of the rope, then spending a very long time fishing for it with a grabhook or grappling iron (a three pronged hook at the end of a rope). The water was always ice cold and usually clear; however at the times that the road, which ran by the front of the house, was being given a new surface of tar and gravel, it caused the well water to taste oily and it would also have a 'rainbow' look to it whilst the work was going on, but it cleared fairly quickly and didn't harm us in any way. Another function for the well was during the summer months, when it was brought into use as a means of keeping the butter, milk and other such items fresh – no fridge of course!

Sometimes, when pulling up a bucket of water, a frog would be swimming in it, and the small creature would be carefully lifted out and gently flipped back into the well – frogs in the well were a sure sign that the water was good and drinkable.

Quite a large proportion of the village had to obtain water this way, although some of the houses had pumps and storage tanks. I never knew our well to dry up at any time, neither did it overflow. Rainwater was collected from the guttering on the roof and, this being a soft water, after being boiled in a large

23

copper, it was used for washing clothes and also on bath nights. On those special nights each week, father would carry in a big old tin bath and place it in front of the fire. My parents would have their baths first, with more hot water being added when necessary and I would be bathed afterwards. Usually, even this water wasn't wasted as – in the summer months in particular – it was used to water the vegetables growing in the back garden.

Also at the bottom of this garden was what my parents referred to as 'the little house' – our only lavatory – and This of course had to be emptied quite frequently. I used to dread having to go outside on what became 'urgent calls' in wet and cold weather and at night-time – especially in the summer months, when all manner of creepy crawlies might be lurking there. There was also the fear of the unknown when it was dark, and I remember my imagination would conjure up all sorts of fearsome creatures that were possibly 'abroad in the night' – especially when I heard any creaking or rustling noises, probably made by rats or mice.

Foxes were frequent visitors to the garden, and whilst these caused us no harm, we none the less kept a sharp lookout for the cats in the family, which, during my childhood, were numerous. When my first birthday was celebrated, I was given a black cat as my own personal pet – he was named Tich – he lived a charmed life, surviving to the ripe old age of twenty one years, before dying of natural causes.

Having no electricity meant that the cooking was either done on a paraffin stove or a solid fuelled range; if you were well off you probably used an Aga cooker. The main problem with the paraffin stove was the smell, but one quickly got used to this – it wasn't unpleasant in any case, and even now I can remember it as a comforting, homely smell.

Paraffin lamps were used for lighting in the main rooms of the house, but candles only were used in the bedrooms. One of the drawbacks of these paraffin lamps was that they were prone to smoke and this made black marks on the ceiling – which meant that the rooms needed decorating at frequent intervals!

I was an avid reader as a child – I still am, but on recollecting all the well known books, with various sizes of print, I read by that flickering light beside me – although it brings back memories of enjoyable bedtimes in childhood, it also makes me wonder now that it didn't seriously impair my eyesight.

I can remember that during those early childhood days, I would often accompany my mother to the shops in the village. In the 1930's there were quite a few shops in the main street, including two grocers' shops, a baker's, a butcher's (which killed it's own meat) and two pubs. The pubs are still there and are still called 'The Griffin' and 'The Rose and Crown.' These are separated by a distance of a hundred yards or so. My paternal grandfather, who was the village molecatcher, could be found most lunch times sitting in the inglenook fireplace of The Rose and Crown's public bar. He would sit there – a pint pot beside him with his pipe burning well and stuck firmly in his mouth – as familiar a sight to the other regulars in those days as the landlord who served him. My father had a preference for the beer that was stocked by The Griffin, but none the less used to take the occasional pint in the company of his father at the Rose and Crown. I can remember my father quite often repeating a favourite saying of his in conversations – "There is no such thing as bad beer – only, some is better than others!"

At the top of the street, was one of the provisions stores, Commerce House; the shopkeeper was Mr. Pollard – a cheery, mustachioed man, who always wore a clean white apron, buttoned to his waistcoat. He was helped in the shop by his wife. I can remember, even now, the lovely smell of the sides of bacon that were waiting to be sliced on the bacon slicer, with its gleaming shiny blade and big red turning handle – it amazed me that he didn't cut a finger off when using this machine. Sugar and currants and other dried fruit, were weighed up during the quieter times and were packed into blue paper bags. Butter was made up into blocks with a pair of wooden butter pats; this was usually done by Mrs. Pollard, as was the cutting and weighing of the cheese. The cheese was cut by using a piece of wire with a handle on each end and I can remember that whilst this was being done, my friends and I, who would be watching the cutting process, almost spellbound, would also be hoping that a small sliver of cheese might be quickly passed down to us – to be eaten immediately and luxuriously by the lucky recipient.

At the lower end of the street was a second provision shop; this was the Post Office Stores, run by Mr. And Mrs. Rumens, who's son, Anthony, like me, would soon be attending Fletching School. They used to employ a Mr.

Hobbs to help them. This being the post office, it was something of a meeting place for the villagers, and the only place where one could obtain stamps and postal orders. Also, as not many of the villagers had bank accounts in those days, a post office savings account was the more general way of saving anything that might be left over from the weekly wage packet, or even from pocket money – perhaps being carefully put by to purchase a new bicycle, more pieces for a train set, or anything else that necessitated an accumulation of cash – too tempting to be left as close at hand as 'somewhere indoors.'

Being an only child, I spent most of my time, in the early years of my life, with my mother – my father, of course, was away at work during the daytime. Before she got married, my mother used to be in 'service' – working for an elderly couple called Jefferies, who had a home at Piltdown, on the outskirts of the Parish of Fletching. Mr. And Mrs. Jefferies also had a flat in Palmeira Square in Hove, and mother sometimes worked there as well. In those days, in the 1920's, there were three postal deliveries a day – even in small country villages. Mother would write and post a card in Hove in the early morning, saying that she would be on the seven o'clock train from Brighton that evening, and father, who was courting her at this time, would receive the letter in time to cycle to Sheffield Park station, also pushing her cycle as he rode to meet her off the train.

My earliest recollection of my father was of a gruff but kindly man, who although christened Thomas, was nicknamed 'Bunny' by most who knew him – they called him this because of his smallness of stature, but to me, at that time, he seemed quite large.

He worked as a sawyer in Sheffield Park sawmills for the firm of 'Albert Turner' – who were based at Sheffield Park railway station. This station, before Dr. Beeching made his redundancies, was on the line that ran between East Grinstead and Lewes, but it's now the headquarters and main terminus of the famous 'Bluebell Line.' He would ride his bicycle to and from work everyday – a round trip of about seven miles. He did this on six days of every week – including Saturdays.

Born in 1890, he had gone to war in 1914, having joined the Royal Sussex Regiment, and soon found himself in France as part of the British Expeditionary Force. He was reluctant to talk of his experiences during what he described as – "those bad times" – but admitted – "I was very lucky to survive some dreadful battles." His good luck continued when he was transferred to the newly formed 'Motor Machine Gun Corps' – in which he learned the intricacies of the Vickers heavy machine gun, and the Clyno and Royal Enfield motor cycle combinations that carried them. After this, he was sent to the middle east, by troopship, with the rest of his battalion. On arrival in Mesopotamia (Iraq and Iran), they were informed that they would be part of the combined Anzac Force, that was going to attempt to land on the beach at Gallipoli. However, he was suddenly struck down with severe dysentery and hospitalised in Baghdad – thus missing being with the rest of the battalion when they were massacred as they tried to land on the beach during that catastrophic tragedy of the first World War. Afterwards, he spoke of some of his time in the middle east – but never of Gallipoli.

In those days there was no industry in the Fletching area and the majority of people either worked on the land or in the saw mill, but on the outskirts of the village there were two estates (Searles and Sheffield Park) that employed quite a lot of local labour – both male and female.

Among my earliest recollections, are the times that I was taken out in my pram on Sundays by my father – thus, giving my mother good time to herself after spending the morning preparing a meal fit for royalty.

Sundays, in those early years of my life, seemed to go on forever, but our ways of life matched this and the ample free time I had was very much appreciated and enjoyed. In the summertime, indeed whenever the weather was fine, I would normally find good activity out of doors, but on rainy days, or when the snow lay thick and the wind blew too cold, I would stay in the warmth of the house, where I was also never at a loss to find something absorbing and enjoyable to occupy the time.

Although the BBC had made their first televised broadcasts in 1930, it would be quite a few years before it appeared as a 'luxury item' in some rather privileged living rooms. The wireless though, was by then a part of everyday life. I can remember one which was powered by a large dry battery and a smaller acid accumulator, that had to be charged up every week. This was done by a man who travelled around the villages in a small van, exchanging charged accumulators for uncharged ones. During the winter, when bad weather, with snowed up country roads, caused him to be late or not to be able to travel at all, the only means of getting the latest news was from the papers, which were delivered by someone from the local shop – or even the postman.

There were no buses to and from anywhere from Fletching during my early years – they first appeared in 1939, more or less coinciding with the outbreak of war. Very few families could afford cars, so bicycles were the main form of transport, although horses were still a reasonably common sight along the lanes and bridle paths. It was a common sight to see young children sitting on special seats installed at the back of their parents bicycles – but only until they could manage to ride themselves.

Most of my pre-school summers were spent in the garden, where my mother could keep a close eye on me, and I shared this 'blessed plot' of ours with the family pets. There were always at least two cats around at that time, including my own black cat – Tich, who was very large – huge, in fact. I also had a goldfish which I kept in a bowl, and had to keep a very discerning eye on Tich whenever he got close to it – I often thought I could detect a glint in his eye at these times.

I was mainly unaware of what was going on in the rest of the country at that time of course, but in later years I learnt that during the year of my birth, 1931 – Mahatma Gandhi, after being released from prison in January, came to England, in the February, for talks and a visit to the textile manufacturing areas of the country. It was also the year that the Labour government had resigned, and a new 'National Government' (coalition) had been formed under Ramsay Macdonald. This new government was to introduce extreme and austere measures in a country already suffering from unemployment and strikes, and harsh new legislation caused riots and even more strikes.

Some other items of news from that year were that the Nazis in Germany had demanded Germany's withdrawal from the League of Nations, the Royal Navy had mutinied at Invergordon – when sailors had gone on strike because of cuts in servicemen's pay – and Thomas Alva Edison, the inventor of the phonograph, telegraph and many devices for the distribution of light, had died; also, at the cinema, Charlie Chaplin in 'City Lights' was drawing in huge audiences.

On reflection of those early days, I think that my most vivid memories are of Christmas times – these special, colourful and festive days of each year were always a time of great excitement to my family and me, and the culinary treats my mother provided for us are almost beyond description in their excellence – she was, quite simply, a marvellous cook. Her mince pies were renowned throughout the local countryside and she won numerous prizes at the Women's Institute. She also excelled at jam making and wine making – the first tasters and judges being father and myself, at home! Later on, during the war years, when the only meat that was obtainable in any quantity – not on the ration – was rabbit, (apart from any 'game' that might have been poached) she could prepare, from this common

31

country fare, dishes that could have been described as of 'Cordon Bleu' standard. Her homemade bread melted in the mouth – she would make two batches of this every week and, considering that most of her cooking was done on a solid fuel kitchen range that depended on wind direction and force, how she produced such marvellous dishes that we always did justice to, still remains a mystery.

Before long my school days would begin, but in the meantime my childhood carried on in a mist of contentment, and I preferred not to think of such things – after all everything was just fine as it was.

Chapter Three

First School Days – Warmth At The Forge

1936 is the first year of my life which I can remember with a fair amount of clarity. This was not only to be a year steeped in the history of this country, but also a very poignant year for me, in as much, that it was when I first started school.

Fletching village school had three classrooms in those days; a small one for the infants, a slightly bigger one for the juniors, called the middle class, and the seniors used the main body of the school, which also served as the dining area. The toilets were positioned outside in the playground.

I was due to start school in the September of 1936, but I can remember that in the days whilst I nervously awaited this new chapter in my life, the general trend of conversation at home was not so much about my future education, as it was about all the happenings in the Royal Family. After the death of King George V, my parents, like nearly everyone else, thought it was just a formality that Edward VIII would accede to the throne; they had read about Mrs. Simpson in the papers of course, but thought that royal duty and the absolute importance of the crown, would win the day – the alternative was 'unthinkable' and they quickly dismissed any other options from their minds. However, events didn't turn out as planned of course, and before long the king spoke to the nation of his love for Mrs. Simpson being too strong for him to consider breaking off the relationship.

The possibility of the King abdicating, now became my parents main topic of conversation in the evenings, and they listened to many of the broadcasts about this awesome time in history; I remember that when a programme came on about this subject, my father would firmly tell me to keep quiet – an order I diligently obeyed!

During these broadcasts, the announcer always seemed to speak in a sombre tone of voice – with an almost reverential intonation.

My parents were staunch royalists and each broadcast provoked much discussion between them – sometimes with minor arguments ensuing. My father thought that Edward was being selfish – "He's putting his own good before that of his country!" – I heard him say more than once. My mother was of a more romantic nature however, and, although she didn't openly take sides, I suspect that her heart was very much with the love story having a happy ending for the couple. I remember that father said that there had been some heated exchanges concerning this subject in the pub when he went there on Saturday evenings.

When the king did finally abdicate, there seemed to be a sense of relief and commenting on this, father echoed what many people were saying, that " – it was a good thing that it was out of the way, and perhaps we could now get back to basics again." He felt very strongly that at a time when there were such ominous political rumbles coming from the continent – particularly from Germany, of course – that the country could now concentrate on making sure that there really would be peaceful conclusions to everything.

In contrast to the abdication, the coronation of King George VI was a joyful and happy occasion and the country felt that it had got the best of the deal. The moods amongst my relatives and their friends, suddenly changed to being almost euphoric and, although there was much drinking of good home made wines indoors, the whole occasion also became a good excuse for 'nipping off' down to the pub for a special toast or three!

In Fletching the coronation was celebrated in similar fashion to the Silver Jubilee of George V, just a year beforehand, and special events were held in Sheffield Park on the cricket ground. There were military parades and bands, and we all sang patriotic songs. Every child was given a toy or a game and a commemorative mug (now collectors items). I remember that my toy was a cork firing pop gun, which I was very pleased to own – although I was told in no uncertain terms where 'not' to aim the cork (with the string taken off), after one or two 'good shots' on my parents – which they didn't appreciate as much as I did!

The whole village was invited to attend these coronation celebrations at Sheffield Park, and they were blessed with fine weather for all the events; in fact it was so dry and warm that during the march past of the troops, they kicked up huge dust clouds – which quickly covered everyone and everything.

In the September of 1936 my first day at school duly arrived. I wasn't too happy about leaving the comforts of my home for this new venture in my life, even if it was only for a few hours each day. On that first day, after much preparation, my mother put me on the carrier of her bicycle and the 'fraught' journey through the leafy lanes to Fletching School began. I remember that on that journey and all the other ones, when she took me to school on the back of her bicycle, I would hang on like a limpet whilst she swayed about as she rode the three quarters of a mile distance of practically traffic free roads. After we arrived, mother stayed for a brief while to see that everything was alright and then left me to my new surroundings – cheering me up slightly when she reminded me she would be seeing me a bit later to take me home. With a lump in my throat, I watched her disappear, but I knew that I had to make the best of it and I was determined not to cry – I didn't – but I came close to it. There were several other children who started on the same day as me, so that at least helped, in as much that they all looked as miserable as I felt!

I don't remember too much about the classes in those first few days of school, but I seemed to settle into the routine of things alright. At playtimes, during the morning, we were each given a small bottle of milk to drink, and I remember that we new pupils spent much of that time keeping out of the way of the bigger children who were involved in the permanent rough and tumble of chasing each other all over the place – for no apparent reason!

It had been planned that I wouldn't have my lunch at school, but instead go to the village reading room, just nearby, where my grandmother was the caretaker. Like my mother, she was also a marvellous cook and there was always a tasty meal waiting for me at this time each day. Afterwards she would walk me back to school, where although the afternoon would carry on in similar pattern to the morning, we were mainly just read to until it was time to go home. I enjoyed this very much – I found it absorbing, and at times, if the story was a very good one, the hands of the clock would turn almost too quickly. At the end of my first day, mother duly arrived to take me back home, where I spent the whole evening telling again and again of all that had taken place on that absorbing, slightly strange, but special day of my life. When it was bedtime, instead of looking at comics by the flickering light of the candle, I was soon into the 'land of nod' and dreaming dreams of strange but not unpleasant happenings, in a world that was new to me, and in what promised to be a fascinating journey of discovery.

During the summer months, we would be taken out on fine days on what were 'loosely' called nature walks. On these walks we would find out about the flora and fauna of the area and, in those days, it wasn't frowned upon to collect specimens and we would arrive back at school with a vast assortment of plants, leaves and other sundry items such as old bird's nests and animal bones and skulls – all of which would be labelled and noted. Being country born and bred was an advantage in matters to do with what grew in the areas near to us – I had also learnt a lot from my grandfather, who was an out and out countryman. He told me where to find such flowers as dog roses, meadowsweet, foxgloves, willow-herb and sweet smelling honeysuckle – particularly fragrant in the evenings; there were also ladies smock, yellow ladies bed straw and, near the river, one might come across wild garlic, with it's unforgettable and pungent smell. We learnt to recognise deadly nightshade at an early age – the glossy black berries, sometimes as big as cherries, which were often called 'naughty mans cherries.' We used to point out stinging nettles to the younger children in the height of the summer and say that they didn't sting in the month of August – they soon found out differently!

At haymaking time in those days, the hay was mostly collected in horse drawn wagons. I remember a small group of us, including my friends Tony Welfare, who lived next door to us and is about the same age as me, Frank Kingsland, who lived just down the road and two other particular friends from the village, John Bradford and Peggy Barton, would spend hours out on the fields getting up to all sorts of games, including – much to the annoyance of the farm workers – constructing our own small haystacks, thus making it impossible to turn it so it could dry out properly before being taken to be stacked. When the hay was dry it would be taken to the farmyard and there made into large haystacks. Once the stack was finished it would be left to settle for a few weeks; after this, the thatcher would roof it with straw, to keep the hay dry – probably finishing it off with a picturesque straw bird or animal as its crowning glory.

As winter approached that year, although I can't say that I enjoyed going to school on every day, I had none the less discovered that it had its good points as well as its bad ones. As I have said, I very much enjoyed listening to the stories that were read out to us – I have always been a keen listener as well a 'compulsive' reader and although I often read comics and similar material before starting school, I know that the roots of my favourite pastime had truly taken shape during those early school years.

During the winters of those years before the war, I can remember seeing snow on many occasions – I was always fascinated to watch it silently fall, leaving a scene that made the landscape look as if it had been transformed by magic.

The Christmas of 1936, like all the other Christmas's of my childhood, went past in a mist of happy excitement and expectation. On waking very early on Christmas morning, just before it got light, I dived to the bottom of my bed, where I knew I would find a pillow case filled with an assortment of mysterious and exciting looking parcels. I had gone to bed later than usual the evening before and during that extension of time, before my bedtime, I had helped mother decorate the Christmas tree – it was a tradition in our family never to dress the tree before Christmas Eve, and my father never used to bring this 'real' Christmas tree home until after work on that day.

Whilst I was playing with my presents, with father joining in with me, mother attended communion at St. Andrews and St. Mary's church in the village. Before going to the service she had prepared the specially bought chicken for the oven – the cooking started the moment she returned and carried on until dinner was served, promptly at one o'clock. During the day there would be a procession of relatives and friends coming to visit us, and a large variety of homemade wines would flow freely, much appreciated for their 'body' and special flavours. My mother was an accomplished wine maker and every year the pantry under the stairs would resound to the popping of corks – when the new season's wine fermented before it was re-bottled and stored. Wine was made of virtually anything that grew in the gardens, hedgerows and fields. Among the many varieties she made were, dandelion, birch, parsnip, potato, wheat, orange, elderberry, blackberry, raspberry, blackcurrent, elder flower champagne and many more, including The one I particularly liked – a lovely golden plum wine.

From the above list, it would seem that we were a family of drunkards, but this wasn't the case because, in those days there wasn't the selection of soft drinks that there are today and while the wine was 'young' it wasn't very strong – just a good healthy drink if taken in moderation. However, when it had matured – then that was a different story!

The wine was left to ferment in huge stone flagons; these would be left uncorked initially and the froth would bubble out of the neck until the fermentation was near to finishing. After this, the corks would be put in lightly – allowing slight fermentation to carry on for a while. Sometimes the corks would pop out of the flagons – a strange sound if you weren't used to it, but if any corks had been put in too tightly, the flagons would burst, with the wine lost.

After all the fermentation was finished, the wines would be bottled; it would be quite funny if the label had come off a particular bottle and you didn't know what flavour you were about to drink until you tasted it – even then, there were some quite heated discussions as to what variety it was!

In the year that I was born my mother had made some wheat wine and put the bottle at the back of the pantry – not to be opened until my twenty first birthday. When that day duly arrived the bottle was opened and the wine sampled and, needless to say, the taste was out of this world and extremely potent   "Enough to make strong men cry!" I remember father saying, although that could have been because there was only one bottle of it!

After Christmas dinner, a slightly tipsy father would do the washing up, before we all settled back to listen to the king's broadcast. The first of these royal broadcasts had been made by King George V in 1932, but the first one that I can remember was the first one made by King George VI. I remember this one in particular because my parents, like many people, wondered how well he would cope, seeing that it was well known that he suffered from having a bad stutter – or he certainly did at that time. I seem to remember that he didn't do too badly on that occasion, although there were some distinct and rather tense pauses from time to time during his speech.

41

In the evening it was party time and the house would be filled to over capacity with grandparents, uncles and aunts and other members of the family. The time would go past in a whirl of talk and laughter, helped along with liberal portions of a variety of special snacks my mother had prepared for the occasion – all, of course, washed down with the much appreciated home-made wines. The 'pieces' de resistance to all this though, were, dads new seasons celery – all crisp and freshly pulled from the garden that afternoon and mothers huge home-made Christmas cake, which would absolutely melt in your mouth – just delicious.

After all this, it would be time to turn the paraffin lights out and light the candles on the Christmas tree. This was done to the accompaniment of 'Oohs' and 'Aahs' from the attentive audience – this also signalled that the time had come to hand around the presents that had been gathering at the foot of the tree since the first relatives had started to arrive. Later on, with the paraffin lights relit and, after many more toasts had been drunk, the relatives started to leave – some of them a little the worse for wear and all of them homeward bound.

Soon after this, with my mind contented and happy to the extreme I went to bed and, with all my new toys surrounding me, I was soon fast asleep.

On Boxing Day morning, my grandfather, who was the local mole catcher, took me for a walk around the village, dropping in to say hello to some of the people he knew. One of the places we stopped at for a while was the Smithy's at Splaynes Green – just near to our house and on the

42

outskirts of Fletching. The smith was Mr. Packham – he was assisted by a Mr. Mundell. I can't think of a more pungent smell than that of a red hot horseshoe being pressed onto the horses foot; it did not appear to hurt or inconvenience the horse in any way. During the cold winter months it was a treat to be allowed inside the smithy's, under grand-dads watchful eye, to feel the heat of the forge and to look into its red depths as it was pumped by the bellows – thus intensifying the heat generated. Mr. Packham was a small man, but he was completely in control of those huge carthorses that were the bread and butter of his trade and still in use in the 1930's and war years of the 1940's and even later than that in places where traditions died hard or pockets didn't stretch to new equipment. The tractors used on the land started to increase considerably in the latter years of the war and would soon, of course, take over 'almost' completely.

Although the arrival of the tractor had spelt out the eventual death knell for much of the smithy's trade from as far back as the late 20's and early 30's, there was still business coming in from the gentry and riding stables and local hunts – even so the trade would soon be drastically reduced – with the craft eventually holding on only by the skin of its teeth, in something of a specialist role.

When tractors replaced the horses on the farms, it also meant that the farmers wouldn't need to employ so many men – the tractor, of course, could do a lot more work in a lot less time, and also, unlike the horse, it didn't need looking after for twenty four hours a day.

My father's Christmas break was a very short one and, the day after Boxing Day, if it was a weekday, he would be back at work again at the sawmill.

The sawmills at Sheffield Park station, where he was employed as a sawyer on the biggest ripsaw, did not specialise in any one thing, but made and supplied the local building trade with all the standard sizes of timber; sometimes though, there would be orders for something different – a one off job.

The big ripsaw that father used was a massive circular saw, which was used for cutting the long lengths of timber that had been through the band saw. The timber would be brought to the saw mill by special timber trailers – drawn by four wheel drive vehicles. These timber 'tugs' – as they became known – were manufactured specially for this job, because of the muddy fields and woods they had to operate on.

The timber yard and sawmill owners were Albert Turner and Son – they employed on a fairly large scale, with several of their employees following in their fathers footsteps at the yard. The site of the sawmill was obviously planned to make full use of the railway system, and a special siding was part of the layout of the works – this ran from the main track.

Just to the north of Sheffield Park station, there are the gardens and lakes of the National Trust property of Sheffield Park, and 'hidden' near the car park for this, are the derelict buildings of the estate sawmill, which would have been equally as large as the commercial one at Sheffield Park station; when the estate had been a thriving one, teams of horses could be seen hauling timber to the sawmill to

44

eventually be used on estate maintenance. In later years the buildings were either converted to other use or simply pulled down.

With my first school holiday coming to a close on a mild winters day in the January of 1937, I found myself being allowed to be just a tiny bit more adventurous in my outings with my friends. One of our favourite pastimes was racing home built 'carts' (converted old prams) up and down the road in front of our houses – there was hardly any traffic at all in those days, and our parents considered this pastime to be safe enough. The carts had been adapted for us – in my case by my father – to have steerable front wheels, and we soon became the 'Nuvolaris' and other such famous racing drivers of that era.

We were getting to the age now, when, before too long, we would be allowed to venture even further away from home, unaccompanied by our parents or other 'senior' relatives and the fields and woodland areas of the 'wild beyond' would soon become our playgrounds and places of adventure during those important years of growing up.

One place in particular that my friends and I used to visit quite frequently, was my Aunt Lucy's shop, about half a mile from us, at Splayne's Green. She had a small sweet and tobacco shop which was situated in the front room of her cottage. As she was unmarried she had to find a job to supplement the money my grandfather would be bringing in as the local molecatcher. All the local children bought sweets from her – she would always add a few more sweets after the scales balanced, making it difficult for me to understand now how she made any profit; none the less, she did! Most of the local men either smoked a pipe or rolled their own cigarettes and, as she was virtually open all hours, she did a good trade in both sweets and tobacco. I got no special privileges here for most of the time, so I know that she did quite a fair bit of trade from me, in supplying me with countless sherbet fountains over the years!

Some of the local areas near to us, would eventually become the training grounds for soldiers that hailed not only from all over the United Kingdom, but also from countries as far away as New Zealand and Canada. The dark clouds of war were already threatening on the continent and the ups and downs of 'misleading' politics would soon break down completely in the well remembered late summer and early autumn of 1939. Before that though, the broadcasts that told of promises of 'peace with honour' and 'peace in our time' were widely listened to and believed by a 'gullibly' hopeful audience who, like my father, had had enough of 'bloody' conflict in the first World War, and who desperately hoped that it couldn't and wouldn't happen again.

I was aware of the conversations about all this of course, but during those well remembered years of 1938 and 1939, my friends and I had other things to think about, and the days were taken up with the time filling adventures, pitfalls and elementary learnings, that were all a part of the pure magic of childhood.

Chapter Four

The Village Bobby – The Miller – War Clouds

With the news from the continent becoming increasingly ominous during the late 1930's, it soon became noticeable that quite a lot of military activity was taking place in the Fletching area, and I remember that whilst I was still attending the infants class, the Territorial Army could quite often be seen holding manoeuvres close by to the school. Once it became known that the soldiers were passing the school, there would be a large number of pupils who suddenly found that they urgently needed to use the toilets – which being in the playground, were very close to where the soldiers passed by and therefore gave us a good vantage point from where to see what was going on. Alas, the teacher soon realised that our sudden requests to answer 'the call of nature' were not strictly honest, and accordingly prevented anyone from leaving the classroom if the soldiers happened to be anywhere in the vicinity and the request to leave the room wasn't a matter of 'life or death!'

On the subject of people in uniform, one character in the village that I can remember very well, for a variety of reasons, was the local policeman – P.C. Cuthbert Meads – who appeared to me to be ten feet tall! He obviously wasn't, but with a helmet added to his large stature – he looked it!

He was respected by everyone in the community, and, more often than not, he dealt out 'summary justice' to anyone, especially juveniles, he caught breaking the law or getting into mischief around the village. If he caught you scrumping, he would give you a cuff round the ear and send you on your way – after telling you not to let him 'catch' you doing it again! Mostly we took this quite literally – in other words, what we interpreted him to mean was – "Go scrumping if you must, but don't be silly enough to get caught!" If he did catch you a second time, woe betide you – but not many were.

Most of us children would refer to him as Bert – but not to his face! He was a larger than life man with an ample girth, who never seemed to be in a hurry but always got the job on hand done – usually with the right result and without fuss.

He first joined the police force in October 1914, when he was 23 years of age, but, like numerous other policemen, he soon resigned in order to join the army after the outbreak of the first World War. He rejoined the police force in the September of 1919 and served the people of Fletching, as their village Bobby, for thirty two colourful years, before retiring on a pension.

In his off duty P.C. Meads was a very good cricketer and the main fast bowler for the village team; also, he had represented the police in other recreational activities and had trophy's as proof of his prowess in the field of sport. In the free time that he had from his duties, he could often be seen in his garden, in his shirtsleeves and braces, hoeing between the rows of vegetables and daring the dreaded greenfly to show itself – he was a gardener of considerable repute.

In those days before the war, the roads of the village were kept tidy and well looked after by a local roadman – called a 'Lengthman' – so called because he had a set length of road to look after. In Fletching, our lengthman was an elderly villager called Mr. Avis – 'Huffer' to us – we nicknamed him this because when he smoked his pipe, he made a loud 'huffing sound as he drew in the smoke. I remember that we boys led old Huffer a bit of a song and dance from time to time – especially in the winter months, when it was one of his tasks to keep the ditches clear of rubbish. We would wait until a certain section of the ditch had been cleared and then block it up with sticks and mud, causing the rainwater to start flooding. We would then tell him what was happening – completely innocently of course! I am sure now, that he must have known what was going on, but being the good natured man that he was, he didn't seemed to mind too much.

On the subject of flooding, after there had been a lot of rain, the river Ouse was particularly prone to flooding – especially near to the mill at Fletching In the 1930's the mill was still in full working order and local farmers would bring their corn to be ground here – returning later to collect the flour. There were lock gates to control the flow of water, and the flow would be diverted to bypass the mill, because the waterwheel would not be able to cope with the river in full flood.

As well as the mill, there were some derelict cottages where the mill hands had lived at one time, and these also figured in our games and adventures in those childhood days. The miller, Joseph Martin, lived in a house just across the bridge from the mill – he was Mr. Martin to us children; we found him to be a very upright and hard working member of the community. It used to amuse us that he was nearly always covered in flour – almost looking as though he had fallen into it! He had huge muscles, which had obviously developed from humping the great sacks of corn and flour about – they weighed at least one and a half hundred weight each.

As a child, it was a treat to be taken to the mill, not only to see and hear it working, but also to see the river; I have always been fascinated by running water, so, when there had been a lot of rain the river would run very swiftly and it was interesting to watch carefully to see what might be being carried along by the speeding water. Sometimes, sadly, it would be the body of an animal or bird, but at other times it could be an out of the ordinary object – something which particularly fascinated us – which the more adventurous of us might try to recover at a suitable place down river.

At times the road would become flooded as well, and the only way to get past the mill was by a clapper bridge; this was a narrow wooden structure, with a hand rail, that ran alongside the road and was about eighteen inches to two feet above the road level and about 120 feet in length – this, of course, was for pedestrians only. It was quite something for us children to stand near here and witness mother nature, in all her fury, sending the river water rushing along the road that we were walking along, quite normally, only the day before. It was a wonder that none of us got drowned, but the worst that happened was that sometimes we got wet, with the water coming over the top of our wellington boots.

During the years that the mill was working, a pastime that was carried out by some of the older boys of the village was – when the mill wheel was turning slowly in its idling mood – the more daring of these boys would jump onto the centre of the wheel and balance on the spindle by 'walking' as the wheel turned. This was a very dangerous thing to do, and if they were caught by Bert, the village bobby, or one of the school masters, they were, usually, quite severely punished. A particular incident I remember concerning the river was when I was watching some of the older boys swimming near to the mill and one of my cousins, who was also watching but standing right by the riverbank, fell in – fully clothed. He was fortunate, in that he was quickly rescued by a grown up – and then, soaking wet and screaming, he was unceremoniously carried back to his home.

The river used to be used for swimming by the boys from the top class at school – usually under the supervision of the headmaster. There was a widening of the river just below the lock gates and this was the main swimming area. There was very little current here, so it was a good place to learn to swim, and also a very good place to fish. The river Ouse held many varieties of fish and was well frequented by local anglers and others from further afield. My main angling years were yet to come, but even at that age I had 'caught

51

the bug' and I can remember keenly fishing for newts in those early days. We used to catch these 'effets,' as they were known as locally, in various ponds and dykes nearby to us – using a stick with a string line, and just a bent pin as a hook. For bait, we would use worms that could be found in the dung lumps on various farm fields – these worms are called brandlings. After catching the newts, we would return them, unharmed, to the water.

The majority of boys in the village were interested in fishing and, when I first started to try to catch something a bit larger than minnows, I would worry my mother to take me, with my friend Tony from next door, to some place that we had a mind to go fishing at – I wasn't allowed to go unaccompanied by an adult. On the days that she agreed to take us, we would cycle to a small river, which was known locally as Daleham Stream – it was named after a fifteenth century house, nearby. This stream, which was too narrow to be called a proper river, none the less held quite a variety of fish in its reaches, and apart from the humble minnows and small fry which were ever present, if you were lucky, you might catch dace, roach, perch, small brown trout or even a 'mighty' pike. In the summer months, in the river Ouse, sea trout would journey up the river from Newhaven to spawn in the quiet, non tidal stretches of the river and sometimes even find their way into Daleham Stream, which originates in Searle's lake and flows into the Ouse just north of Goldstrow Farm at Piltdown. Over the years, try as hard as we did, we never caught one of these treasured fish, which are also called 'pink salmon' – maybe this was just as well, because it was against the law to take them out of season. However, I was told that poachers, out to earn a bit of extra cash, were known to use a bright light to attract the fish at night and then net them, or even shoot them – although I can't see that a fish that had been shot by something like a twelve bore shot gun would be left in a good enough condition to be sold!

In later years, when I was allowed to go out with my friends, there would be many 'nefarious' adventures to the private lakes at Sheffield Park – but more about those adventures or misadventures, later on.

I can recall going out with my grandfather quite a lot during those pre-war years – he seemed to me to be extremely old – he was actually in his late seventies. He was a small man, who was kept busy in his trade as the local molecatcher. In those days there were men like him in most villages – moles were apparently a problem to farmers, as well as on cricket pitches and peoples lawns. To catch them, he would set a series of traps, and each day he would go and inspect them and remove and keep any moles that had been unfortunate enough to get caught. These, he would skin; afterwards curing the skins – which would eventually be made into various forms of clothing. Moleskins, being a warm and quite hard wearing material were turned into a variety of things – many a gentleman, in those days, would wear a moleskin waistcoat for Sunday best; I had a moleskin suit when I was about two years old, and my mother had a moleskin fur coat, which must have taken many moles to produce.

My grandfather was well known to all the local farmers, and he made a reasonable living following his trade. Like most other men who worked on the land, he would wear a striped collarless shirt – called an Oxford shirt – also, thick corduroy trousers tied at the knee with string, they called these 'Yorks' – they were held up with a wide leather belt, and in most cases, braces as well. In the winter a woollen 'Gansey' – a type of jersey – would be worn under a heavy serge jacket. On his feet he always wore a pair of heavy hobnailed boots, which had to treated with dubbin every now and again to keep them waterproof and supple. During the weekdays he would never be seen without his familiar cloth cap, but on Sundays he would wear a battered brown trilby hat.

Grandfather was also a keen observer of the wildlife of the area, and often took me with him to watch some of the many aspects of nature during my holidays. He knew where to find many different kinds of birds nests in the spring and would know the lairs and living places of many of the wild animals that abounded in the woodlands and lush pastures of the countryside that surrounded us.

Unfortunately, at the same time that the position in Europe was looking particularly ominous, grandfather caught a chill, which soon took a very firm and critical hold and quickly worsened – he died just before that fateful day in 1939, when we were told that we were at war again. I couldn't understand his death – it just didn't sink in at first, and I often expected him to 'just turn up' and take me on one of those enjoyable nature rambles.

I missed him very much, but, on reflection now, I can only say how lucky I was to have had such a tutor in the ways of the countryside, at such an impressionable age.

I never knew my maternal grandfather, Frederick Newnham, he had died several years before I was born; he was a carpenter and builder and well known and appreciated locally, for the work he did. My paternal grandmother, Louisa Butcher had died in 1919, but my mother's mother, Lois Newnham, Frederick's wife, who was caretaker of the village reading room and who lived in the reading room cottage, I saw a lot of – she was very close to me. She was very well known in the village and did a lot of much appreciated community work. Every year she would organise an event which went under the name of 'Pound Day' – this was a special day when people from the village would bring pounds of sugar, tins of meat and fish and other such groceries to the reading room; these would then be taken to the local hospital, The Uckfield Cottage Hospital, to help out with their food supplies. Many people would contribute a sum of money instead of groceries, but whatever the donations were, they were always very acceptable.

Before the war, medical care was private – this, of course, was in the days before the National Health Service; however, there was a scheme whereby families contributed a few pence every week to cover emergency health expenses and call out by the doctor. Most local doctors made up the medicines that they required for the patients, themselves – this was also in the days before penicillin and antibiotics. I remember that most of the medicines seemed to be highly coloured and, from experience, they usually tasted pretty foul – a lump of sugar certainly did help the medicine go down! I also remember that after bath-time on a Saturday night I was given a spoonful of sulpher and black treacle or a dose of syrup of figs – quite a few households swore by this 'preventative measure' – it was usually successful in keeping us 'regular!'

Boils were fairly prevalent in those days, but were awkward to treat – especially amongst the younger section of the community. The usual treatment was to bathe the affected area with water, as hot as the patient could stand, several times a day; in between times the area would be covered with a poultice, to draw the poison out. When one was attending school with this affliction, the head teacher would have to carry out the treatment during the day, and the older boys would sometimes be called upon to hold the patient whilst the treatment was being administered. I suspect that this 'duty' wasn't mentioned when the teacher applied for the job.

Childhood illnesses, such as measles and mumps, would sometimes cause whole classes to be absent from school at the same time. A frequent visitor to the school in those days was 'Nitty Nora,' the nurse who inspected children's head for lice. We all lined up quite happily for this time consuming attention, because it meant less time doing lessons – surprisingly she only rarely discovered the presence of lice!

In the papers on May 29th 1937 the headlines had told of Mr. Neville Chamberlain becoming the prime minister of the new coalition government, and also told of appointments to senior positions of many well known figures in the political arena of that time. My father, commenting on this, said – "We could do with a good shake-up in the government, let's hope this lot can do better!"

By this time I had accepted school as a part of everyday life, and actually enjoyed quite a lot of what went on – although it still had its 'down' times. During the rest of that year life carried on much as before and I remember that the summer seemed to last forever – one more of the wonderful summers of childhood. Christmas and New Year also passed enjoyably and, as young as I was, I felt that life was very good – I was more than comfortable in the bosom of my family.

In the late 1930's it had become noticeable in Fletching, Piltdown and many other rural areas – especially on the farms – that there were quite a few 'refugees' seeking work. These unfortunate people, had thought it was wise to get away from Nazi Germany and any other countries likely to become scourged in the shadow of the swastika – where the Jews, Gypsies and various political outcasts were now 'persona non grata' and in danger for their very lives. It turned out that many farms, on the eventual outbreak of war, were only too pleased to employ this extra labour, especially a little later on when the land needed as many hands as it could get because of new government legislation to use every available piece of land in order to grow much needed food for the country.

During the early months of 1938, the situation on the continent hadn't improved much and there was still the fear that we might go to war, but in The Sussex Daily News on Thursday 29th September 1938 the headlines told of 'Eleventh hour hope for peace – historic meeting at Munich.' After this meeting at Munich, which had been at Herr Hitler's invitation, it looked as though there really would be 'peace in our time,' and I can remember my parents expressing their relief at this news. However, although the outlook had now become much more hopeful, at a time when many people had taken it for granted that another war was just around the corner, another article in The Sussex Daily News was headlined 'Precaution work goes on in Sussex 'and under separate headings which said – 'Reception of London refugees' and 'census of accommodation proceeding – distribution of respirators almost completed.' The article went on to say – 'All the work in connection with air raid precaution in Sussex was in full swing yesterday when Mr.Chamberlain's announcement of a further conference with Herr Hitler, in conjunction with Signor Mussolini and M. Daladier became known.' Later in the article, the newspaper reported that gas masks were being issued in parts of Sussex and, amongst other things, told of window frames being reinforced against possible bomb blast – in other words, despite all the encouraging signs for peace, we still weren't going to be caught with our trousers down!

I can remember when we had to go to collect our gas masks quite well, and during the early months of 1939, when the position on the continent looked very much worse, we were taught what to do in the event of there being an air raid or gas attack. At home, once again the talk was of the 'probability' of war, and consequently we started to prepare ourselves for the worst. I remember my father spoke of people he knew who were already making enquiries about joining up in one of the armed forces and he told mother that this might make a difference to the work force at the sawmill, although he thought that there would be many, including those on the land, who would be required to carry on with the necessary work that they were already doing. Father had done his bit in the First World War, and in any case, in 1939, he celebrated his forty ninth birthday and was therefore beyond the age of being called up again.

Amongst those from the village who were soon to be called up was a character called Fred Gladman – known as 'Radicker' to quite a few people. He was employed as an under-keeper on the Sheffield Park estate, and one of his jobs was to break up some ground near the head keepers house, so that the frost could get into it and break it up further. For some reason, the head keeper called this job 'radicking' and, as Fred would often tell people that he had been out 'radicking' that day, the nickname Radicker soon stuck. He was a familiar sight in the village as another one of his jobs was taking the teams of horses from the estate, to be shod at the smithy's at Splaynes Green and this would often be watched by an appreciative audience, mainly consisting of us children. Another story concerning him that comes to mind, is about a farming relative who quite often invited him and his wife to Sunday lunch. The lunch was always the same – meat pudding! Fred's relative would cut the first sizable portion and put it on a dinner plate; then add plenty of vegetables and gravy, and then give it to the dog – saying that if the dog hadn't done his work properly that week, then there wouldn't be any meat pudding on the table!

In a conversation with Fred recently he also told me about one of his first jobs on leaving school. He was a gardeners boy for a time, at Searles Estate – working for the Maryon Wilson family. The lawns, in those days, were mown by a donkey pulling a mower – this was before the days of motor mowers. To stop the donkey's hooves from damaging the lawn, leather shoes were worn by the donkey. Putting these shoes on could take a long time, or just a few minutes – it all depended on the mood of the donkey! If it wasn't possible to fit the shoes quickly then Fred would wait for half an hour or so until it was in a better mood! "Something else of times gone by that no-ones ever likely to see again." Fred said to me.

The summer holidays of 1939 didn't seem much different to any of the other holidays to me, except that as each year went past I found myself venturing further afield than before, and I was now getting to know the areas that surround Fletching quite well. I had celebrated my eighth birthday early in the summer and, accordingly, I had been given just that little bit more 'licence' in my activities.

During the long days of my holidays, I remember that the wireless seemed to be on for quite a lot of the time; my parents, like most people in the country at that time, expected that important announcements about the situation worsening on the continent, might come at any moment. When it was eventually announced that Mr. Chamberlain would speak to the nation the following day, Sunday 3rd September, I remember father remarked about a Sunday being an odd day to address the nation on, but supposed that this in itself was extremely ominous, and that it seemed "the writing was already on the wall!" However, I also remember mother saying "Well – there's always hope isn't there?" – and with those words very much in their minds, my parents prepared themselves for the broadcast, whilst fervently, but not very optimistically, hoping that there still could be a peaceful solution 'around the corner,'

Saint Andrew's and Saint Mary's Church Fletching

Mother, Father with me (just arrived)

Grandfather (the village molecatcher) in his regular seat
at The Rose & Crown Fletching

and in his sunday best

The Mill, Fletching, Sussex.

Fletching Mill – in the days when horses delivered and collected the corn

The funeral of Lord Sheffield

66

Cricket match on ice – Sheffield Park 1902/03

Sheffield Park Gardens

My early interest in camping

and

The hopeful flyer

Sheffield Park Station – 1912

A group of friends – just to prove that we did allow girls to play with us – sometimes!

Chapter Five

Evacuees – Some Arctic Weather – The Battle of Britain

The thing that made Sunday September 3rd 1939 a very different sort of a Sunday for me, was that I was told by my mother that we wouldn't be going to church that morning and this meant that the choir, which I was a member of by that time, would be short by at least one voice. I can't remember whether I was pleased or disappointed by her decision, but what I do particularly remember about that morning was that there was a feeling of apprehension in the atmosphere of the household and my parents tenseness in waiting for the all important announcement to be made by Mr. Chamberlain, had certainly given me a feeling of insecurity, or, to put it more plainly – I felt frightened!

The morning was a beautiful one with plenty of sunshine and hardly any breeze; it was also very warm and as I played in the garden, before the broadcast, I noticed that the windows of both the cottages were open wide and the wirelesses from both of these could be plainly heard. At just before eleven o'clock, my mother, who had been keeping a special watch on the 'outside world,' as well as me, that morning, called for me to come indoors. A few moments before Mr. Chamberlain came on the air to speak, I remember father saying, "Well here we are, all keyed up and fearing the worst – but let's hope things aren't as bad as all that !" I felt even more apprehensive when I heard Mr. Chamberlain begin to talk to the nation, and I also remember that when he confirmed that we were at war with Germany, my father loudly and angrily 'exploded' with the words, "Damn – we're bloody well at it again!"

Things seem to happen in something of a frightening blur after this; within minutes, the air raid siren sounded and my mother grabbed hold of me and pulled me under the dining room table with her – to shelter from the bombs which she thought might start falling at any moment. My father stayed where he was and continued listening to the wireless – "I'm not letting any Germans, particularly Adolf 'Bloody' Hitler, frighten me!" He said loudly – but he didn't discourage mother and me from seeking the best form of shelter we could find on the spur of the moment.

Many people had prepared for the war and the possible eventuality of air raids, by building shelters in their gardens, but father used every square inch of our back garden for growing his 'prized' vegetables, so we had to find the best shelter we could indoors. He had also reasoned that it probably wouldn't be necessary to build a special shelter, seeing that we lived right out in the country and the air raids – if there were any – would most likely be on specific targets, such as towns, cities, ports and military establishments – " – Hardly likely on isolated houses in quiet country lanes!" He also reasoned.

It wasn't much more than ten minutes later when the all clear sounded – nothing had happened and the rest of the day passed peacefully. I stayed very close to my parents after the broadcast and I remember that father didn't even go down to pub for his Sunday pint – which, in itself, was most unusual. A little later we went to see my grandmother and the conversation, of course, was all about what might happen next, or how long the war might last, and so on.

That night, although I went to bed a little apprehensively, I none the less slept well and when the next day and the days that followed stretched on without any signs of our being attacked by the enemy, my fears were lessened considerably and life carried on in much the same fashion as it always had. My parents listened out for news of what was going on on the continent and at home much more regularly than they had in peacetime years, and the newspapers were absorbed more thoroughly than usual. On the 30th of September, after nearly a month of inactivity, one article in our daily paper, summed up the situation as follows:

'After a month of anxiety, false alarms and uncertainty, Britain is settling down for a wartime winter. The government had expected 100,000 casualties during the first few weeks of the war. Hospitals had been cleared, mortuaries stacked up with piles of cardboard coffins and lime-pits dug to cope with the dead. Every home has a hand operated stirrup pump and long handled shovel to deal with incendiary bombs. Memories of the Spanish civil war and Guernica were still fresh.

74

But the Blitzkrieg did not happen. Instead, Britain is being bombarded by regulations and petty officialdom. Public information leaflet, number one, urges everyone to carry a luggage label with their name and address. A national register is being completed and identity cards will be issued by the end of next month.

As they stumble home through blacked-out streets, avoiding vehicles with dimmed out headlights, Briton's are fast becoming used to air raid wardens shouts of – "Put that light out!" Giant posters have appeared urging the populace to save, dig, work, buy war bonds, not travel, not waste – nor spread rumours – all for victory!

The blackout is total, with the shops long since sold out of blackout material. Householders are urged to paint the edges of their windows black – even the slightest chink of light can lead to heavy fines. Road deaths have doubled, forcing the government to ease vehicle lighting restrictions – head lamps had to covered with cardboard with two inch wide holes, and allow only one headlight to be lit.

Commuters glow an eerie blue in dimmed railway compartments, while unlit buses caused chaos to drivers and passengers alike.'

In the country, on the roads, the thing was to try to avoid going out on bicycles after dark, but if your journey really was necessary, muffled lights were the order and it was useful, of course, if you had a good knowledge of all the twists and turns, ditches and any other impediments that were on the route you were travelling.

At home, it had by now definitely been settled that the best place to shelter in the event of an air raid was in the pantry under the stairs. This was now cleared of everything that was not essential to be stored in a cool place, and the geography of this arranging also made it essential for us to have plenty of blankets and things to keep ourselves warm – hot water bottles as well if it was extremely cold. Inside this small space, mother had put a collapsible bed, which was just big enough for me – she sat on a stool whilst sheltering with me. If the siren had gone before it was my bedtime, then I would go straight to bed where I was, otherwise, I would stagger sleepily and somewhat unwillingly downstairs, whilst hoping that the duration of the raid would be a short one and I would soon be able to return to the comfort of my bed upstairs. It was a strange feeling, sleeping under the stairs – rather like living in a cave. Also, there was a 'winey' smell there that became stronger during the summer months; this came from countless stone bottles that wine had been put in to ferment during the wine making seasons before the war and it had permeated the brick floor. Whilst there, we had the added feeling of security, that should a bomb fall on the house and trap us, at least we would have plenty of food close at hand. Whilst we were sheltering in our 'cubby hole', father would go outside for some of the time, to see if there was anything that he could see going on in the way of enemy activity in the area.

At school, a large 'blast' wall had been built just outside one of the main doors – by the boys cloakroom. The boys and girls cloakrooms were both used as shelters, each sex sheltering separately, but the infants all sheltered together in the small cloakroom outside their classroom.

From the moment war had been declared, children, quite often with their mothers, had started to be evacuated from areas likely to be bombed – London, in particular of course. Fletching was to take its share of these evacuees or 'Vaccies' – as they became known. We were allocated a mother and her small child – we had a room in the attic which was suitable to hold a bed and cot, and which was really quite cosy.

On the day the evacuees arrived – in Fletching's case, in coaches from the east end of London – a central reception area was set up in the reading room, so my grandmother was very much in the forefront of the organising when they first arrived. For the Fletching families that did take in evacuees, the choice of who they got was made for them and they were allocated according to what space they had – so, it was all very much pot luck!

Many of the children had never ventured further than the neighbourhood they had been born in and consequently many things in the country, came as quite a shock to them. For instance – discovering that milk came out of cows and wasn't just 'something' that was bottled! Quite a few children refused to drink it, on discovering its true source.

As I have said, quite a number of the evacuees had arrived in family groups – in other words a mother with children or just one child – but, within moments of arriving, many of the mothers expressed there shock at finding that there were no 'fish and chip' or 'eel and pie' shops in Fletching, and quite a few of them refused to stay and went back on the same coach.

Things were quiet in London at that stage in any case – it was still the 'phoney' war and it would be another year before the 'Blitz' would make the evacuation of many children, much more urgent. At that time however, several of the mothers said that they'd sooner face the bombs, rather than go without the necessities of a life style that they'd been born into and which had been passed down through countless generations.

Our particular evacuees found the countryside much too quiet for them and, after three days, they decided to return to London. After a couple of weeks or so there were only a 'handful' of children left from the several coachloads that had first arrived. Those that did stay fitted in quite well – although there were a few fights with the locals, which were soon patched up and forgotten about. The evacuations may have worked well in some parts of the country, but for Fletching it was mainly a 'non event' and, although quite some effort was put into the planning, there hadn't been too much thought of how the enormous change in lifestyle might affect those that had had to sacrifice the sanctity of their homes, in order to stay alive.

The big estates in the Fletching area – Searles and Sheffield Park – were soon taken over by the war department and converted into army camps; the largest of these being in Sheffield Park. When the first of the army regiments arrived here, although guards were placed at the entrances to this camp, it was, none the less, very easy for us kids who knew the area well, to cut across the fields and gain entry by quite a choice of places.

The first soldiers to occupy the two estates were members of The Royal Army Service Corps, who had the job of getting the camps ready for other regiments. They lived under canvas until the permanent quarters had been built. After this, The Royal Artillery then took up residence in Sheffield Park; they were equipped with batteries of 25 'pounder' guns, which were pulled by four wheel drive tractors, called 'Quads.' Other troops to come here at this early stage of the war, included detachments from The Royal Corps of Signals and The Royal Army Medical Corps. These were later followed by the New Zealand General Army Corps, and eventually – the Canadians.

From our early adventures across the fields to the camp at Sheffield Park, where we were hardly ever questioned about what we were doing there, we soon got to know the makes of the lorries and motor cycles they used – as well as all sorts of other details about what was going on there. We had even got to know what the password to gain entry into the camp was – later on, there was quite a fuss made about this! I remember father saying – "A spy wouldn't have to get into the camp to find out about things – all he'd have to do is ask the local children!" However, we did get lectures in school, as well as from our parents, about careless talk costing lives and so we became very secretive about anything we saw on our adventures – also, any strangers to the village were treated with great suspicion by us.

The weather in October and November 1939, was very wet, but by late December, heavy frosts were a prelude to a period of extremely cold weather, with more severe frosts and eventually – plenty of snow.

The first Christmas of the war passed quietly for us, it's a Christmas I can't recall too much of, although I do remember that during the peacetime early years of my life, it had always given me great pleasure to go outside when the Christmas tree lights were lit and watch them from there for a few minutes – but now this wasn't possible because of the strict blackout laws.

In the harsh winter of early 1940, I can particularly remember a day when it seemed that everything had turned to ice – in fact it became known as the 'day of the ice storm.' The roads were literally like an ice rink and icicles hung from everywhere – even the leaves of the evergreens were encased in ice, as were the branches and trunks of trees, where the lashing rain of the night before, had frozen as it landed. There were icicles of all shapes and sizes and I remember hearing father say that it wasn't so much a winter wonderland as a winter nightmare! He also said that it was a good day for staying at home – but none the less, he went to work. My most vivid memories of that time, are of the telephone and electricity wires being coated with a thickness of ice that was heavy enough – in some cases – to bring them down to the ground, and cut off supplies. Many of the wires that weren't brought down, looked like ropes of jewels hanging there. Also, vegetables soon became scarce because the ground became too hard to get them out – this, of course, didn't help the food situation, taking into consideration the austere wartime rationing we were expected to live on at that time.

Conversations about the war on the continent, now took second place to the 'very English' subject of the weather. Back on January 17th, it had been reported that the Thames had frozen over and at that time also, we noticed that all the lakes and ponds near to us had frozen over thick enough for it to be safe to skate on them – plenty of locals, as well as people from further afield, took advantage of this – the most popular place locally for this winter sport, being Piltdown Pond.

However, on the 28th of January, the skating had to stop for a while as an enormous blizzard, during the previous night, had left the snow too thick everywhere to even find the ice – the papers described this blizzard as the worst storm of the century! During the harshest of that weather, when the temperatures were at their bitterest, many schools throughout the country had to close because of burst pipes and freezing classrooms – Fletching School was one of these. It was an enjoyable time for us children – not only were we having time off from school, but we were busily enjoying that time, sledging and snowballing. Nearly every family had a sledge of some sort and, as there were plenty of hills nearby and, as the roads in those days had very little traffic, we could play for hours without interruption.

When we eventually returned to school, after the pipes had been repaired, the main entertainment was snowball fights. These were forbidden in the school playground owing

81

to the stony nature of the surface making it dangerous but, none the less, I can remember on one occasion, when the local roadman was walking by the school and his head could be seen showing just above the top of the wall, that this proved too much of a temptation for some of the senior boys and, all of a sudden, snowballs were flying thick and fast in the direction of the moving head – quite a few snowballs found their mark and this resulted in several boys from the top class getting caned.

My first turn for getting caned was still a little time away, but when we did get caned it was on the hand. However, there were various methods that were thought might stop it hurting too much; these methods included, having orange peel rubbed into the skin and another one – 'an old wives tale' – was to place a horsehair on the palm of the hand; it was said that this would split the cane – it never worked!

Stories of all sorts of incidents concerning the weather reached us through the village 'grapevine' or through father at work. Some doves were found frozen to the roof of a house at Maresfield and we were told that sheep had to be dug out of deep drifts on the downs nearby and others had to be extricated when their wool had frozen to the gorse bushes that they were seeking some form of shelter by. Our local milkman managed to carry on delivering by horse and cart – the milk arriving later than usual, but arriving none the less. We also heard of other milkmen who were delivering by sledge in some areas.

The thaw eventually arrived in late February, causing some local flooding – I can remember that I had never seen the river by the mill looking so fierce and forbidding before.

In May, I can remember that during what seemed to be permanent days of sunshine, the news was full of the plight of the British Expeditionary Force in France and Belgium. For many days the news told of amazing rescues from the beaches of Dunkirk, but this time the war had not only become the main topic of conversation again, but also, as matters were of such a critical nature, my parents, like so many other people, now followed the news on the wireless, almost hour by hour. I found everything very frightening; I couldn't help overhearing some of the conversations between my parents or other adults and these conversations gave me the impression that not only was there the very real fear of our being invaded by the Germans, but also that it was likely to happen – very soon!

Before long though, the good news was that hundreds of thousands of troops had been rescued by a fleet of little ships that ranged from fishing boats and motor cruisers to pleasure steamers and of course the destroyers and other ships of the Royal Navy. It had been a miraculous rescue, which was accomplished by both military and civilian personnel, and it meant that we now had all those troops back to help defend our shores, in the event of being invaded.

Just before Dunkirk, on May 14th 1940, Anthony Eden, the war minister, broadcasting to the nation, asked for volunteers to help defend the home shores, particularly our own local areas. These volunteers, which he emphasised were 'urgently' needed, were, at first, to be known as the

Local Defence Volunteers, but the new prime minister, Winston Churchill, soon had this changed to, 'The Home Guard.' He also insisted that these volunteers should wear proper uniforms, instead of – "just gallivanting about in a variety of civilian togs."

At first, it wasn't only the uniforms that they lacked, but also the weaponry, and they could often be seen parading, or standing guard, armed with just pitch forks, broom handles, or – if they were lucky – shotguns.

Fletching had its own Home Guard Unit and my father was very quick to volunteer for this – especially because of his experiences in World War I. The Home Guard was mainly made up of men too old to join up again or too young to have been called up yet; there were also other volunteers for this from those with reserved occupations, such as in farming – those who were able to find the time. There were even some who, although they were slightly disabled, were still considered fit enough to take part in some capacity.

Each night, the members of the Home Guard, including my father who had quickly been made up to corporal, took it in turns to patrol the village – especially if there had been an air raid warning. Ammunition was scarce, so in training, to make the appropriate noises, they would use thunderflashes – rather like Christmas crackers, only considerably more explosive and without being really dangerous. During the time The Home Guard were 'operational,' there were several places where they met up – including the roadmans hut on wheels and the local reading room where my grandmother was the caretaker. There was also a local branch of The Auxiliary Fire Service, which had a trailer pump towed behind a very ancient car. Most houses kept buckets of sand in case of incendiary bombs – some were even issued with stirrup pumps, but not us.

During the high summer months of 1940, we, at Fletching, as in so many places in the south east of England, were to witness many aerial battles fought in the clear blue skies all around us.

The weather during June and early July 1940 was what is best described as variable – with a lot of low flying cloud, intermittent light rain and, from time to time, periods with clear blue skies. Later on in July, the clouds thinned and it marked the beginning of a period of beautiful summer weather – weather, which at normal times we would have enjoyed to the full in the fresh air and countryside surrounding Fletching. Unfortunately however, this weather also made it possible for the Luftwaffe to increase their activities over England – particularly over Sussex and Kent. Enemy aircraft now ventured further afield and, what had been mainly 'skirmishes' over the channel, now became intense aerial warfare above the towns and countryside of south eastern England. The Battle of Britain was about to begin in earnest and we were soon to witness many of the amazing fight sequences that would soon be occupying 'centre stage' in the skies above us. This of course was a time of high anxiety – not made any the less frightening by the general feeling that this was probably the prelude to the home shores being invaded. What we didn't know then though, was that Hitler had planned that during the period 15th–17th September, 'Operation Sealion' – the invasion of Great Britain – would be put into operation.

During those beautiful summer days of July, August and September, although the air raid siren might go at any time, my friends and I still ventured out on fishing expeditions to nearby stretches of water and I felt I was becoming quite proficient in this sport, even if I was still only catching tiddlers rather than monsters. Sometimes, without any warning, while we were out fishing, 'dog fights' would materialise in the sky overhead and, within seconds, the antagonists would disappear – leaving behind the white whispy strands of exhaust fumes, clearly marked against the sheer blue of the sky as the only evidence of the battle that had just taken place.

Before 'Operation Sealion,' was to be put into effect, Hilter's plan was for the Luftwaffe to attack the airfields of Fighter Command – in other words they hoped to destroy many aircraft whilst they were still on the ground. They had some success in doing this, but they didn't by any means achieve what they had set out to do, so they eventually changed tactics and decided to send large numbers of aircraft to bomb London, in particular.

By August 10th a huge force of German aircraft, a larger force than they had ever mounted before, were set to attack the home shores. For a while though, they were prevented from launching this attack because of cloud cover, and it wasn't until August 12th that we noticed that the Luftwaffe were far busier than usual – with one air raid following another throughout the whole of that memorable and terrifying day. Our pilots were, of course, trying to intercept the German aeroplanes before they got to London and this resulted in many aerial battles taking place over the fields and towns of Kent and Sussex – particularly, it seemed, over Fletching and nearby areas. We witnessed many battles taking place all around us and saw several aircraft, both German and British, trailing smoke after being hit – but we didn't actually see any crashing to the ground. Later on, on the wireless, we were told of what casualties there had been and, for the Germans, these were considerable; we were also told that although they had attacked and damaged six of our vital radar stations – only one had been put completely out of action.

These attacks set the pattern for some time to come and, whilst we watched as much as we could from wherever we were, never knowing what might happen next, we fervently willed on our pilots to victory – sometimes cheering loudly and hoping that even if they couldn't hear us, they might at least see us – they were that close to the ground.

In the weeks that followed, there were so many aerial duals in the skies above Fletching that my friends and I soon became quite proficient in recognising aircraft from the sound of their engines – the British Merlin engines of the Spitfires and Hurricanes, and the Daimler Benz of the German aircraft – each with their own distinctive sound.

The war in the air was also to provide a means of collecting souvenirs, such as, machine gun and cannon shell cases that fell to earth. I remember on one occasion, whilst out walking with my mother we had to take shelter in a farm building whilst a dog fight was taking place overhead – this was half way between Fletching and Splaynes Green. There was a lot of gunfire for a short while, then everything went quiet again and we resumed our journey home. However, before we had gone many yards we started discovering the spent cases of some of the ammunition used in the battle – there were shell cases dotted about all over the place. I picked up as many as I could carry and the next day took some of them to school with me to swap for anything that I hadn't already got, with other collectors.

During the latter part of the summer holidays of 1940, we came to expect these aerial activities throughout the long days of leisure – I remember father reading out one report from the newspaper, early in September, which said that the Luftwaffe had made no less than thirty three raids over southern England between August 24th and September 6th – but it seemed like more than that to me.

We were kept informed by the newspapers and the radio of most of what was going on, including the numbers of enemy aircraft brought down, but what we didn't know about was that since 31st August, Spitfires and Hudson Aircraft of Coastal Command had been returning with 'impressive' photographic records of the number of barges and other invasion craft in the ports and estuaries across the channel. It was recorded that in Ostend on August 31st there were just eighteen barges standing in readiness, but by September 6th this number had increased to more than two hundred of such vessels standing by for this ominous purpose.

Another thing that happened at this time, that not many people knew about, was that on the night of September 6th, an alert had been sent out to people in command of various sections of the Home Guard, saying that the invasion was imminent! In one of the papers a report included the following " – In the prevailing excitement of receiving this alert a few commanders of the Home Guard units rang church bells to call on their men, thus spreading the impression that German Paratroops had actually landed!" On hearing about this later on, my father said he was very pleased it didn't happen at Fletching or anywhere else nearby that was within hearing distance. None the less, he remembered it was a very tense time for all the members of the Fletching Home Guard once they had been made aware of the alert. In his case there had been a knock on the door in the middle of the night – or certainly well after he had gone to sleep – so he had got dressed and joined the others at the roadmans mobile hut, just down the road.

Also later on, when father was telling us about that night, he said – "Everything was very quiet, apart from occasional sweeps of aircraft going overhead, and from time to time we could hear barrages of anti-aircraft fire in the distance. We really thought this could be it, but it all quietened down by the morning. None the less we were still on full alert, but with instructions not to talk about anything that was going on, of course – this would have caused panic, something we wanted to avoid at all costs!"

A day or so later, father also told us about an uncle of mine, who was also in the Home Guard. Apparently, members of the Home Guard who worked on remote farms, were given permission to carry rifles and were issued with live ammunition for them as well. My uncle worked on a farm near to the Ashdown Forest and the village of Hartfield. During one of the dogfights, he saw a Heinkel 111 which had been damaged and was flying very low with smoke trailing from one wing – it was coming straight at him – so he took a shot at it. The aeroplane eventually crashed some distance away, but he never found out how accurate his shot was – the plane was probably doomed in any case!

The alert carried on for a quite a number of days after this, during which time we witnessed dogfights galore in the skies over the Fletching area.

The last really big day of The Battle of Britain was September 15th, when mass attacks were mounted by the Luftwaffe in a last desperate bid to gain supremacy in the air and inflict severe damage on strategic targets and anywhere else they bombed. During that day, the enemy lost at least sixty aircraft – the British, no more than twenty six, with thirteen of the pilots saved. It was another big German defeat – 'the last straw that broke the enemy's back.' By the 17th September, Hitler was left with no alternative but to postpone Operation Sealion indefinitely and a few days later he ordered the dispersal of the invasion craft.

The Battle of Britain was over, but the clear blue skies of that beautiful Indian summer remained as a reminder of a summer – the likes of which we had never seen before, and hoped we would never see again!

As a nine year old, all of what had happened had given me a lot to think about, but on reflection, although the summer of 1940 had been fraught with danger, I am glad that I was there to witness this amazing time in history.

Before long though, the night raids would begin and the sirens would blare out all too frequently during the autumn and winter of that year and for several years to come. The war was still in its infancy and in the months and years ahead of us, we would see much more of the many activities of a war that was to affect us all and remain a part of our lives – impossible to forget.

Chapter Six

'Dubious Supplies' – Visitors From Overseas

In the months that followed the Battle of Britain, although we at Fletching saw and heard some of the action that was going on over the south east of the country, for most of the time the heavy bombardments were mainly over the London area, in what had come to be known as 'The Blitz.' There were many reports in the newspapers which kept us reasonably well informed about what was going on but, of course, there was also heavy censorship. One particularly disturbing report appeared in a Sussex 'local' paper on Monday 7th October 1940, just when we were putting The Battle of Britain to the back of our minds; the report was headlined – 'Blitz' Resumed – Big Battles Today' – the article went on to say – 'After the quietest night since the beginning of the air blitz, the Battle of Britain flared up again today when terrific air battles were fought out between British and Nazi fighters.' However, this report was a bit over the top, and the raids after this certainly weren't on the general scale of the Battle of Britain, but came mainly in the shape of fairly frequent bombing raids. Fortunately, articles as depressing as that one didn't appear too often; mostly, even if it was 'propaganda,' the reports tried to keep an optimistic note in them.

As far as we were concerned, in Fletching, the skies were nothing like as busy and threatening as they had been during the Battle of Britain, although now and again we could hear or even see quite a bit of activity going on in the distance – especially towards the Newhaven and Brighton areas.

By now the threat of imminent invasion had lessened and, apart from the occasional scare, when another aerial battle took place somewhere near to us, or when there was a bombing raid, life carried on much as usual.

When the night raids began, I can remember being woken up in the night to take shelter under the stairs with my mother and, at first, these raids were quite frequent and often very frightening. Fortunately for us, although we could hear a lot of the bombing activity going on, it was mainly in the distance – there were many raids when we heard the warning siren and later the all clear, with 'nothing' in between. In those early weeks during the blitz, it seemed that I spent an awful lot of time in that tiny space under the stairs; fortunately most of this time was spent sleeping!

It was at about this time that a few more evacuees started arriving in the village, to get away from the horrors and the nightmare of the blitz in London. Things were very different there now and the air raid activity had 'warmed' up considerably since the early days of evacuations. These evacuees mainly settled in quietly and without much complaint – this time having made suitable arrangements with whoever they were going to stay with, well in advance of arriving – no more leaving it to pot luck!

At school, during the Christmas term of 1940, most things carried on in the same way as they had at the end of the summer term – only this time there was the excitement of the run up to the festive season to come.

In November, we had once again missed our firework display in the garden. In peacetime, my father would set fire to a guy made from worn out old clothes and stuffed with straw and mother would serve baked potatoes, oozing with butter, to a small crowd of neighbours who had brought their fireworks with them to add to ours and make a good display. Mulled wine was served to the adults, whilst we children enjoyed delicious homemade ginger beer.

Nearby, at Lewes, they used to host the biggest firework display in the country, with magnificent processions of people, from different Bonfire Societies, parading through the streets in highly colourful costumes – they still hold these special celebrations there to this day, but although I never went to one of these special nights before the war, I can remember being taken to the recreation ground at Fletching, to be shown the glow of the torchlight processions in the distance. Now, everything was dark, not a light to be seen anywhere; heavy clouds covered the stars that would otherwise have given some relief in a bleak wartime scene that's best described as – eerie, forbidding and desolate!

Just before the Christmas of 1940 there was a lull in the activities of the Luftwaffe – almost as though it had been

94

'specially arranged' for the festive season. However, although this was much appreciated at the time, the bombing started up again the day after Boxing Day.

The build up to the second Christmas of the war at home, was different to the first one, in as much that, because of the rationing and scarcity of many of the foods that normally adorned our table during the festive season, these 'luxuries' were now – either impossible or very difficult to obtain.

Mother had started saving up portions of dried fruit and suet to make the Christmas pudding and had also been putting by small amounts of 'bits and pieces' from our rations, in order that, at least, the Christmas period would be different to the austere days of the rest of the year.

Recipes had been published by the Ministry of Food; some of these included using such things as carrots in cakes and puddings and dried eggs now substituted for fresh ones – although, being in the country, we did get a reasonable amount of new laid ones. The fresh meat ration was 'held over' for several weeks before Christmas, so that it could be added together, in order to buy a large chicken – a luxury!

This was a time when rabbits became a staple part of our diet, and variously cooked fresh country fare frequently appeared on our table. It was obviously a time when the local poachers managed to line their pockets more than they would normally have done, but no questions were asked – people were just glad to get the extra food. There is an old Sussex proverb that says 'The people of Fletching live by snapping and ketching' – which implies, that even in more peaceful times, plenty of poaching went on in the area.

During the war, the blackout must have made it easier for this 'nefarious' activity to increase in momentum and because of the dire rationing, there weren't many who would refuse the chance of purchasing a pheasant, partridge or hare, making sure not to ask, " – from whence it came?"

The 'established' poachers had many ways of catching their quarry, and a very good knowledge of where birds could be found roosting on the branches of various trees and bushes – places that they could find almost blindfolded – the dark was no obstacle.

The Christmas trees we had at home during the war years were actually holly trees – the real ones, that were usually harvested in quite large quantities for Christmas, weren't grown in any quantity during the war, the space was needed for growing food. This didn't mean that there weren't any Christmas trees – just that there weren't anything like the amount that there were in other years; however, we found that a holly tree was a good substitute and looked most attractive when decorated.

At tea-time, we celebrated in much the same way as on pre-war Christmas's, with all the relatives arriving for this highly enjoyable annual event – despite the different circumstances and wartime restrictions. Even during the wartime, mother would still make delicious bread and, with fathers home grown and freshly pulled celery, it still tasted really good – even without any butter, because of the tiny amount we were allocated from the rationing.

There was still some wine left in the house to celebrate with, but not as much as usual. The sugar rationing had very nearly put an end to mother's wine production – unlike in peacetime when she would make wine out of practically anything that grew, and which was always well appreciated. However the pre-war stock was fast diminishing – although there were still some bottles that mother kept for very special occasions and the Christmas of 1940 was one of those. So, despite the austerity, the toasts were still drunk, and the guests went home, at least mellow, and certainly happy!

On Friday 27th December, the papers headlined that the Christmas 'lull' in the war was over and that the long range guns, now situated on the French coast, had started shelling Dover again. Our local paper confirmed that during the three previous days Britain had been free from air raids. However, when the air raids did start again, it seemed to be the big towns that were getting the worst of it, whilst we, in the country at Fletching, escaped most of this activity and remained unscathed. None the less, the air raid siren did blare out quite often, especially at night, so I still found myself sheltering under the stairs quite frequently.

On Monday 20th January 1941, the headline in the Brighton Evening Argus, said – 'Five Raiders Down Last Night' – and went on to say ' – one crashes in flames on Sussex farm.' We learnt later that this was just a few miles from us. In the years to come, we would hear of, or even witness, aircraft coming down not too far from us, but up to this time the only 'crash' had been a spitfire that force landed near a power line – about three fields away from the recreation ground. The pilot was unharmed, but, as this was quite a long time before we would get used to seeing such fighter aircraft quite frequently taking off and landing in the distance – at what would become Chailey Airfield – this aeroplane proved to be something of a 'novelty' and people were curious to see what a spitfire looked like close up. I remember that just about everyone from the village flocked to see it, and even obtain souvenirs.

There was plenty of snow again during the winter months of 1941, but it wasn't quite as bad as the year before.

On Tuesday 18th February, the local papers told of widespread air raids on Sussex coastal towns and we later heard that Eastbourne and Brighton had had bad air raids, causing some quite extensive damage – with loss of life. During the rest of 1941, whilst the war still raged on – seemingly with most of the action going in Germany's favour – things were rather grim, but the papers and the radio kept us fuelled with information about what was happening on both the home front and also overseas, as optimistically as they felt they could – although, perhaps some of this was only just short of blatant propaganda!

In May we heard the depressing news that the British ship, H.M.S. Hood, had been sunk, but just a few days later the news was more cheering when we learnt that the pride of the German navy, The Bismarck, had also been sunk.

On 1st June, we were told that clothing was to be rationed, but that workmens overalls, as well as hats, caps, mending wool, elastic, suspenders, garters and other such things, including all second hand clothing, would remain coupon free.

During most of the rest of that 'dark' year, the news from the battle fronts was anything but encouraging and the outlook was grim. However, on 22nd of June, the news came through that Germany had invaded Russia, and it was some comfort to know that Hitler's attention had been diverted in this direction – particularly, as my father pointed out – "Napoleon had come a cropper when he tried to do the same thing!"

Back in May 1941, I had celebrated my tenth birthday; I had achieved double figures at last – it was an important day for me. During the summer holidays that year, I was allowed to go out with my friends and explore deeper into the areas surrounding Fletching. We quite often went fishing at places I had never fished before – there were plenty of these in the area. One of the places we explored and also tried fishing at, was Sheffield Park and the lakes there – this was now, of course, in the hands of the army. The New Zealanders who had been stationed here for a while, would soon be leaving – the following year they would be in the thick of the fighting at El Alamein. My parents had made friends with one of these soldiers, Jack Sands, and they often invited him home for a meal. He told us many fascinating stories about New Zealand, but the thing I remember most about him was when he was at our house on one particular day, it snowed, and he just stood at the window watching it, as if he was spellbound – he had never seen snow before! Later on that year, after the New Zealanders had gone, the Canadians started to arrive – we were to get to know quite a few of these tough looking soldiers, who amongst other things, would soon be training for the ill-fated raid on Dieppe.

I think at this stage it would be appropriate to put in here an account about the Canadians and the regiments that arrived at Sheffield Park and Searles, from October 1941 until late 1944. This account appears in the Fletching Parish 'Book Of Remembrance' – dedicated to the men of the parish and the Canadians and others who gave their lives during the 1939–1945 war, who were also associated with the parish. I will come back to 1942 after this informative piece in the book, which is headed – '1941–1944 – In grateful memory and appreciation of the 6,000 Canadian soldiers who were stationed in Fletching parish before seeing action in the Mediterranean and North West Europe:

'After the fall of France in 1940, and with the build up of our own and other commonwealth forces in Britain, suitable training areas had to be found. It was only a matter of time therefore, before Ashdown Forest became a training area and units of the Canadian Army began to be stationed in the surrounding towns and villages. Later, the area being close to good ports, was ideal for units preparing for the battles to liberate Europe.

Thus began the association between the parish of Fletching and Canada. For the soldiers, our parish was often the last home they knew before they went into action in Sicily, Italy or France. They were here at a time of great peril to this country and have an honoured place in this book of remembrance.

The first unit arrived in October 1941, Le Regiment De La Chaudiere, a French-speaking infantry battalion raised in

Quebec. They established a camp in Sheffield Park, using the entrance that now serves the National Trust Gardens from the Lewes Road.

Within a short time, two adjoining camps were located in Sheffield Park: The Lewes Road camp, already mentioned, and a 'Fletching Village' camp, approached through the Lodge Archway in the village. In January 1942, the 4th and 105th Anti Tank Batteries of the 3rd Canadian Anti Tank Regiment, Royal Canadian Artillery (RCA) were the first to move into the 'Fletching Village' camp. Corrugated iron Nissen huts had been erected on concrete bases in a sea of mud. There was no water, no electricity, drainage or roads until April 1942,provided mainly by unit self help. Some of the rubble for the road building came to Sheffield Park from bombed sites in London. Life was not comfortable, but one soldier wrote "How good the people of Fletching were to us. There were houses with little W.V.S. signs in the window and you could arrange to have a bath there. We always left our soap behind." (Soap was scarce for civillians in 1942.) Another wrote "The publicans of Fletching, Piltdown and The Kings Head deserve medals and wound stripes." Sheffield Park House had become a Headquarters, Royal Canadian Artillery by April 1942 and contained a NAFFI canteen and a YMCA reading room, where films were also shown. Brigadier Guy Simonds, later to command the 1st and 5th Canadian Divisions in Sicily and Italy, and the 2nd Canadian Corps from Normandy to Germany, was billeted in the Sheffield Arms. The camp Commandant throughout was Brigadier Eric Snow. Both Le Regiment de la Chaudiere

101

and the 3rd Anti Tank Regiment, as part of the 3rd Canadian Infantry Division, were to be among the first to land on the beaches of Normandy on D-Day, 6th June 1944.

In April 1942 there was a complete changeover of units, with the Cape Breton Highlanders moving into the camp previously occupied by the French Canadians. The Battalion also had one Company at Searles, and stayed until the spring of 1943. At the same time the 17th Field Regiment RCA, moved into the 'Fletching Village' camp, but only until August when their place was taken by the 5th Light Anti Aircraft Regiment, RCA. A bronze plaque in the church commemorates their stay:

This plaque is placed here by the 5th Canadian L.A.A. Regiment, R.C.A. in appreciation of the privilege of worshipping in this church.

August 1942–March 1943

A member of the Regiment remembers that during their stay, their camp was machine gunned by a German aircraft. (During the war, within the parish, two bombs fell just south of Sheffield Park; incendiary bombs on and around Woolpack Farmhouse; sticks of bombs along the A272 and between Holmesdale Farm and Northall Farm, and two bombs on Flitteridge Farm. Also an American Flying Fortress (B17) crashed in the fields just beyond the Recreation Ground; a Messerschmidt 109 close to Tinkers Wood, and a Spitfire at Gold Bridge).

The 8th Field Regiment, RCA, equipped with self-propelled guns, arrived in February 1943 and departed in July of the same year. The Cape Breton Highlanders and all three Artillert Regiments were part of the 5th Canadian Armoured Division and fought in Italy, and later in Northern Holland as part of the 1st Canadian Corps.

In November 1943 there was the second and last, complete changeover, with units arriving who were to stay until they left for Normandy in July 1944. The 15th Field Regiment, RCA, composed of the 17th Battery from Winnipeg, 95th from Calgary and 110th from Broadview, shared Sheffield Park with the 5th Anti Tank Regiment, RCA, whose Batteries were the 3rd from Gananoque, 65th from Grenfell and 96th from Edmonton. We know that the 17th Battery was 'near the gate on the Lewes Road', with the 95th and 110th 'along the shores of the lake.' The officers were 'across the fence from the Manor House.' Both Regiments were part of the 4th Canadian Armoured Division of the 2nd Canadian Corps which fought from Normandy to Germany. The whole of this division must have been in the area, as they held a parade of the Division on the 17th May 1944 on a 'common near Forest Row' for the Canadian Prime Minister, The Right Honourable Mackenzie King, who was met by a Guard of Honour followed by a drive past of tanks, artillery, half tracks and trucks of all kinds, row upon row and eight abreast. The parade was followed by a Drumhead Service on 'an historic sports field' (Lord Sheffields cricket pitch?) in the lines of the 5th Anti Tank Regiment in Sheffield Park.

It is also recorded that a VI rocket exploded near the Sheffield Arms on 17th July 1944, the night before 15th Field Regiment, RCA, left for France. No one knew what it was until the next morning when intelligence reports stated '27 pilotless planes were over London last night.'

After the two Regiments departed, the camps were used for training Canadian Infantry reinforcements and finally, in August and September 1945 they became Canadian Repatriation Depots.

At a conservative estimate, at least 6,000 Canadian soldiers stayed in the Parish for varying periods between October 1941 and September 1945. All too many never returned to their homeland.'

During the times we went fishing at one of the lakes at Sheffield Park, whilst the Canadians were there, the grounds were also still 'protected' from poachers by a game keeper – an elderly gentleman, who wasn't exactly 'fleet of foot.' However, we concealed ourselves as best as we could from him – even if we did know that we could easily outrun him, should he discover us. It must have looked strange to him, or anyone else passing by, to see one of the bushes by the lake with a long stick pointing out of it, several feet over the water – the bushes were thick enough to give us good cover and make us 'invisible.'

With all the military activity going on at the park, when it was known that a battalion or regiment were about to leave the camp, we children would descend on those troops like a horde of locusts and take anything that they didn't want to take with them. This could range from anything such as tubes of toothpaste to items of clothing and various other odds and ends – one soldier even left his rifle, but after something of a 'hue and cry' about this, it was soon recovered.

The Canadians mainly smoked their own brands of cigarettes – the most popular of these being called 'Sweet Caporal.' Many of us were already keen collectors of various items connected with the military – such as cap badges, discarded shell cases and shrapnel; the Sweet Caporal cigarettes now provided us with one of the most popular collecting items of the war. On the backs of these cigarette packets were printed drawings of all the aircraft taking part in World War II – from every country involved in the war. So, the collections included aircraft from Germany, Japan and Italy as well as from Britain and America.

These cards were printed to help the troops in aircraft recognition and were an education in their own right. They showed what an aircraft looked like from head-on, sideways and underneath. It soon became a common occurrence for the Canadians to be approached by some child and asked – "Got any Sweet Caporal backs mister?" Invariably, these soldiers, most of whom smoked, would tear the backs off their empty packets before discarding them and save them for the children. The 'craze' of collecting these cards soon spread and there weren't very many kids, in the areas where the Canadians were, that didn't follow this hobby. I can remember it was hugely enjoyable comparing collections with friends and others and hopefully swapping duplicates for cards that we hadn't got. I kept my collection for quite a few years after the war, but sadly, I no longer have them.

In the papers on Friday November 14th 1941, the headlines told of the sinking of H.M.S. Ark Royal, our most famous aircraft carrier – she was sunk in the Mediterranean, east of Gibraltar. Although, fortunately, the casualties weren't very heavy, this was, none the less, grim news. However, on the 7th of December, the Japanese attacked Pearl Harbor, and that meant that this effectively brought the Unites States into the war against Germany as well – Japan and Germany being the two main partners of the axis power. Although this was terrible news for the Americans, it none the less gave us in this country the feeling of not being so alone any more and meant that we now had an extremely strong ally – even if we were an ocean apart from one another. In their murderous attack on Pearl Harbor, the Japanese had awoken a sleeping giant and although the world situation looked grim at the time, the feelings were optimistic as to the actual outcome and it looked as though the evil forces of Germany and Japan could well have bitten off more than they could chew!

On Wednesday 10th December the papers reported that the battleship H.M.S. Prince of Wales and the Battle cruiser H.M.S. Repulse, had been sunk by Japanese aircraft whilst trying to defend Malaya from attack. With this and other bad news seemingly coming in most of the time, our spirits during the festive period of 1941 were toned down somewhat, but Christmas was still celebrated in the traditional way.

By this time the austerity from the food rationing was making it difficult to find the extra luxuries we looked forward to at this special time of the year. However, with careful provisioning and saving up of rations, mother still provided an enjoyable variety of food, and we knew that there must have been many who were far worse off than us.

Also, by this time, the Canadians were making good use of the locality, in as much that when we had an extremely cold spell of weather and the lakes and ponds were all thickly frozen over, they played impromptu games of ice hockey on them. I remember seeing them playing this game on Piltdown Pond – quite a crowd of us gathered to watch them. Also, I was told that when the ice was at its thickest, during the most extreme cold, they even drove jeeps on the pond.

At Christmas time each year, during the time the Canadians were here, the children of the area would be invited to Christmas parties at the camps at both Scarles and Sheffield Park, with each child being given a gift – usually of sweets or chocolate. To thank them for their generosity, we would put on a show for them at the school, in the New Year – I think they appreciated this, it reminded them of their loved ones at home and, just for a while, made the war seem far away.

During 1942, I progressed fairly well at school and found myself really quite enjoying most of the lessons. Although I continued to have my dinner at the village reading room

107

with my grandmother, I can remember one particular incident that happened during the summer term of that year which was to do with school dinners. One of the boys refused to eat his dinner one day; he said it looked awful and would make him sick, so he adamantly refused to eat it! The teacher wasn't having this, so the boy was made to stay sitting at the table until he had eaten the now congealing mass in front of him – he was still sitting there when it was time for the afternoon break! During this break the teacher was called away, and whilst she was gone, the boy tipped the whole lumpy mess into the top of the school piano. A bit later the teacher returned, and seeing the now empty plate, told the boy he could rejoin the class – after washing the plate. Several weeks later there was a dreadful smell coming from the vicinity of the piano and, in the end, a piano tuner was called in to investigate. He decided that the mess he discovered in the piano was a dead rat – which having got in there, was unable to get out! No one, at that time, discovered the truth.

Another thing that I can remember from those school days is that sometimes during lunch times a child would somehow call the teacher out into the playground, and whilst she was there, one of the bigger boys would rush into the school and put the clock on five minutes – enabling us to get out of school that bit earlier at the end of the day. Eventually this ruse was 'rumbled' and the clock was put out of reach of anyone – without using steps.

In my free time, my friends and I were still venturing out on many missions of discovery in the local countryside, but the place that we frequented more than anywhere else – where we weren't supposed to go – was Sheffield Park Estate, where the Canadians were well settled in and busy getting up to all sorts of things in their training programme. The lakes at the park were used for landing craft and small boat training, and the extensive grounds were also ideal training areas, because of their varied terrain. Our secretive visits to Sheffield Park, now became more frequent, because, apart from collecting Sweet Caporal cards, we also 'added' to our collections with anything else we found just laying around – seemingly discarded and which took our eye.

In the early days of the Canadians being at Sheffield Park, hardly anyone questioned what we were doing there, but by going there in small groups, we at least tried to remain reasonably inconspicuous. Considering the things we got up to, especially during the long summer of 1942, it's a wonder that some of us didn't get injured – or worse!

The twenty five pounder guns couldn't be fired in the camp, so small bore rifles were fitted to them, so that they could simulate the actual firing. We soon discovered that boxes of ammunition were kept by the guns, and if we removed just a few rounds from each box, they weren't missed – or certainly no one came searching for them. We would remove the actual bullets from the cases, and then put the cases in gate hinges – and then shut the gate, thus causing the detonation caps to fire. Another bit of mischief we got up to with these cases, was to put them in the coke pile that fuelled the school stoves – causing some considerable explosions when the stoves were lit. We thought that this lark was particularly funny, but it wasn't long before it was discovered what was going on and the ammunition was also put out of reach.

In the village, on some evenings after the pubs had closed, there would be pitched battles between the French Canadian soldiers and troops from other Canadian Regiments – there was intense rivalry there. When these melees were in full swing, the military police would arrive in lorries and wade into the fray with battons swinging and throw those that they could get hold of into the trucks and take them back to camp.

The best benefits we got from these generous soldiers, were the sweets – or candy, as they were collectively called by them. This, of course, helped out with our meagre sweet ration of eight ounces a month, and we became the grateful recipients of such luxuries as butterscotch and chocolate. They also gave away plenty of chewing gum, we thought it was quite the thing to be seen chewing vigorously, just like some of the film stars in the American films we used to go and see.

During the period of time between April and August of 1942, we noticed that the Canadian Regiments at both Sheffield Park and Searles, were now intensifying their training procedures. What no one knew was that early in April it had been decided by those in high command and senior government, that the pleasant holiday resort of Dieppe, on the French coast – a direct link with Newhaven in Sussex, had been selected as a suitable target for a sea-borne assault. It was to be a combined operation, British and Canadian, on a much greater scale than anything previously attempted, or, as Churchill put it, " – a way of testing the enemy's defences – a reconnaissance in force!"

The idea for such an operation arose, not only out of the British determination to 'harry' the enemy whenever and wherever it might be possible, but also as a 'rehearsal' for the eventual invasion of the continent from the United Kingdom. It was thought and hoped, that, at least, they could discover what sort of resistance would have to be met in the endeavour to seize a port on the French coast.

Thousands of Canadians, many of whom were stationed at Sheffield Park and Searles, took part in this ill feted raid, which was commonly and rightly termed a 'bloody' disaster; I know many who would criticize this ill judged catastrophe in far stronger language than this!

We immediately noticed the stunned atmosphere at Sheffield Park – especially when some of those who had taken part returned to their camps. We particularly noticed the downcast faces and general air of tension, and after we had learnt of some of what had taken place, we trod warily and, for a time, our visits to Sheffield Park became far less frequent.

At home the atmosphere also seemed rather gloomy, and I remember that the conversations between my parents were anything but optimistic about the outcome of the war. However, on October 23rd the news came through of the campaign in the desert starting to swing in our favour, with the Eighth Army advancing under the command of General Montgomery and, most importantly – victory at El Alamein.

111

After this famous victory, the papers were proclaiming that this could, at last, be the turn of the tide. At home, the atmosphere, after all the gloom and doom, suddenly became almost euphoric and I remember that at least a couple of mother's treasured bottles of home-made wine were opened in celebration. I also remember that father went to the pub shortly after the news came through, and found it difficult to get to the bar. He later told us that it had been a really happy evening there and that, at last, there was a general feeling of hope in the air.

In a speech made by Mr. Churchill, just after El Alamein, he said that although this victory was not yet the beginning of the end, it could at least mark – "The end of the beginning!" These words seemed to sum up what most people were thinking, whilst also hoping that it wouldn't be too long before there was some light at the end of a very long and very dark tunnel.

Me and my second bicycle

Waterfall on the river Ouse at Barcombe Mills

and

Browns Boathouse – also at Barcombe Mills

114

1. Sheffield Park Station in the days of steam

2. Sheffield Park Station
(Timber Yard is behind station nameplate)

Father in the Home Guard

Me relaxing in a nearby meadow — in the height of summer

Piltdown Pond

Cricket match against comedian Jimmy Edward's Handlebar Club.
I am standing third from the right

Jimmy Edwards getting close attention at the wicket

Chapter Seven

A Crash – A Character – Victory In Europe

Throughout the war, Fletching village and surrounding areas didn't suffer too badly from the effects of the air raids. The first bombs to fall close to us were three fields away and, although they didn't make very big craters, I particularly remember that on the morning after they fell, there were children and even grown-ups, collecting pieces of shrapnel from all over the place – many pieces, quite some distance from where the bombs had fallen. There had been quite a lot of reports of people being killed by 'flying' shrapnel during air raids, but I'm glad to say that there were no local casualties reported.

During this period of time, many of the games we children played had wartime connections to them and we would quite often re-enact bits from films we had seen – with everyone eager to be the hero! We would get up to all sorts of things and often play tricks on each other – or, more probably, on those we didn't know too well. One of the tricks we played, which was later to have a sinister side to it, was called – 'See the German's head.' A box, large enough to contain a human head, with the words – 'See the German's Head' –

written on top of it, was displayed with the added words – 'A Penny a Look.' There were usually quite a few 'customers' among those who weren't familiar with the trick, but all they saw, on opening the top of the box, was a German postage stamp with Hitler's head printed on it. We all thought this a very funny game to play, and even some of the grown-ups laughed with us, but this harmless trick was seen in a very different light after a cousin of mine, who lived in the village of Hartfield, on the Ashdown Forest, actually did find a German airman's head just near a crashed aircraft. He got into a great deal of trouble about this – he had even put his 'gory' find into a box and was actually charging a penny to view it! He was apparently collecting money, unselfishly, for the local war weapons week!

During the winter of 1942/43, there was some snow, but not as much as the previous few years. However, it was during that festive season that we found ourselves frequently humming or whistling to the tune of 'White Christmas' – this famous song was on everyone's lips and was, of course, a smash hit for Bing Crosby. Other popular hits of that year were – 'This is the Army Mr. Jones,' 'White Cliffs of Dover' and 'Deep in the Heart of Texas.' Popular films doing the rounds at that time were, 'In Which We Serve,' written by and starring Noel Coward, 'The First of the Few,' starring Leslie Howard and 'One of Our Aircraft Is Missing,' starring Hugh Williams and Godfrey Tearle. Out of Hollywood came 'Mrs. Miniver' which was set in England, as the Americans saw us at the time, but which was, none the less, an excellent film. We went to see all of these films and thoroughly enjoyed them.

It was early in 1943 when we heard of another Spitfire crashing not far from Fletching – this one, unlike the first one when the pilot had been unhurt, was sadly different though. The aircraft was in a power dive at full throttle and didn't pull out of the dive – it buried itself forty feet deep in a nearby water meadow and the pilot's body wasn't recovered for several years.

The nearest enemy aircraft to crash, was just north of the village. This aeroplane was a Messcherscmidt 109, that had come off the worse in a dog-fight with a Hurricane – the pilot, who was uninjured, surrendered to some villagers.

Whilst writing of aeroplanes that crashed or had to come down anywhere they could – near to Fletching that is – the most significant one that I can remember was when an American B.17, Flying Fortress, force landed one afternoon in a field adjacent to where the Spitfire had come down earlier in the war – not far from the recreation ground. The aircraft had been on a mission over Germany and had sustained quite a lot of damage – including one of its engines being put out of action. It had circled the area looking for a suitable place to force land and, eventually, it belly landed in a nearby field – its undercarriage still retracted. We had been following the aircraft's progress on our bicycles, which meant that we were among the first at the crash sight. Luckily the ground was fairly soft and the plane didn't catch fire; it had successfully avoided some nearby power lines and finished up beside a hedge. Several

123

of the crew were injured, including one airman who had a piece of shrapnel hanging from his cheek – one of the other crew members pulled this out and quickly dressed the wound for him. Before long the authorities arrived on the scene, but before their arrival we had managed to 'obtain' some of the used cartridge cases and other small souvenirs – some of these I treasured and kept for many years. There was some difficulty in moving the aircraft from its position in the field and it had to be dismantled into manageable sized portions – even the hedges had to have gaps made in them and various gates also had to be removed, before they finally succeeded in getting it all away.

An area close to the village, that I haven't mentioned in any detail so far, is called Shortbridge. This is really just a cluster of buildings and a mill which stands on a tributary of the Ouse, to the north west of Isfield – between Piltdown and Uckfield. The mill was owned by the Maryon Wilson family, who also owned quite a large part of that area. In 1841, it is recorded, that the mill was occupied by Ann Packham, widow of Joseph Packham – the Packhams were well known Sussex millers. The present mill at Shortbridge is just north of the road bridge over the stream and carries the date 1871 – it is now empty. Very near this bridge there is a cave cut into the sandstone rocks – within fifty yards of the road junction to Isfield, Uckfield and Piltdown, at a place called Buckham Hill. Every village has its 'characters' and the one that I can remember most clearly from those times, was called 'Molly Mothballs,' who, for quite a period of time, took up residence in this cave. She used to travel around the roads of the area, pushing an old pram, which contained all her worldly possessions. Although she was a harmless eccentric, she frightened us children – probably the fear of the unknown. Another thing that didn't exactly endear her to us, was that she never seemed to seem to change her dark clothing – just added to it in cold weather. She could often be seen sitting near to a conker tree, near where Alexandra Cottages stand – she used to call this tree her own.

She got her name because she used to keep a supply of mothballs with her – she simply liked the smell of them. Some people thought that she used to sell them, but I don't believe that this is so. Badger Balcombe, who used to be a local resident at that time, told me that he didn't think she sold anything, but simply relied on 'being looked after' by some of the locals. I feel though, that she might well have picked and sold some of the wild fruits of the countryside and sold these. Badger also remembers that she was the last person he saw as he waited to catch the bus at Piltdown, to join the army – unfortunately, he wasn't to see her again. On one dark night, during the war years, she had been wandering the country lanes and had been run over by an army lorry. It is something of a local mystery as to exactly when she had first appeared in the area or where she had come from, but I can remember someone saying that it was thought that she came from a well to do family in the Brighton area and, for some reason, had opted out of society – a sad but colourful little episode in the history of the area.

At this time during the war, we were still getting air raids from time to time, and I can remember hearing and seeing German aeroplanes passing overhead, on their way to bombing raids over London – we seemed to be in their flight path. I was later told that the spire of Fletching church acted as a land mark for the German pilots. Sometimes we saw planes caught in the beams of the searchlights – one of which was positioned about a mile from our house. During the light hours, the raids seemed to be less frequent, but I can particularly remember one daytime raid when my mother and I were walking home from school, and an enemy aircraft came down low and appeared to be flying straight for us – we had to dive into a ditch – a frightening experience! There were several of these low level attacks at that time; during one of them, a train travelling from Lewes to Horsted Keynes, was 'shot up' – with several of the passengers injured.

In July 1943, it had been noticed that on the outskirts of the nearby village of Chailey, a large amount of airmen were engaged in levelling a space of ground. It was thought that they were getting ready an area, large enough to be a new airfield – this speculation turned out to be correct. For some time now there had been a lot of guesswork about when an invasion might be launched from the home shores, on the occupied coast of France, and there was also much speculation about where, on that large coastal area, the landings were most likely to take place. The favourite, the place that immediately came to most peoples minds, was the Pas De Calais – the closest piece of France to England.

However, this was also most likely to be the most heavily defended area as well, so the speculation continued.

It was felt that it was obvious that the build up of troops, including the Canadians and Americans, as well as those from other countries, including the Free French, were a sure sign that the invasion was imminent.

In May 1943, the news had come through that Tunis, in North Africa, had been captured by the allies, who by this time were showing their superiority in the desert campaign. Also, there had been the news of the famous 'Dam Busters' raid on the great dams of Germany. On July 3rd it was reported that the allies had invaded Sicily. With all these good pieces of news coming in, it was now felt that invasion day was indeed imminent. However, what wasn't taken into consideration by the 'layman' was the huge amount of preparation that had to be done before this critical assault could take place.

Back in 1941, plans had been formulated for the attack on Europe – it was called 'Operation Hadrian' and it was decided, at this time, that there was a need for at least six more airfields in the Kent and Sussex area. In 1942, Chailey had been named as one of several sites that were thought might be suitable as ALG's – advanced landing grounds. A preliminary survey had been conducted in early 1942 on farm land forming part of the Hooke Estate near Plumpton Green, and the sight was accepted at a meeting of the air ministry on June 30th 1942. Work had been started to prepare the ground as an airfield by the Royal Engineers Airfield Construction Unit, on 28th October 1942. For some reason there was a delay after this, and it wasn't until the following year that two flights of No. 5004 Airfield Construction Squadron, approximately 150 men, were engaged in levelling the ground – this lasted from the beginning of July to the end of September 1943. By this time word had filtered through to us at Fletching of what was going on, but something that wasn't found out about at the time, was that a report dated 30th November 1943 had said that the airfield was immediately 'operational' – subject to delivery of materials. As far as we were concerned, what looked like a new airfield seemed to have been constructed, but now, nothing much seemed to be happening there and we, more or less, forgot about it for a while.

The rest of 1943 passed mainly quietly for us, with Christmas and the New Year spent in similar fashion to other wartime festive seasons. The winter of early 1944 was generally a mild one and our sledges hardly saw the light of day.

On 25th/26th/27th April, 1944, several Polish squadrons, including nos. 302, 308 and 317 squadrons, were the first Spitfire Squadrons to take residence at the new Chailey Airfield. The staff of 18 Wing H.Q. which had moved from A.L.G. Deanland, near Golden Cross, also took up residence, and Chailey Airfield became – 131 A.L.G. The farmhouse at Bower Farm became No 131 Airfield Headquarters and Westlands Cottage in Bower (now Beresford) Lane was the operations room and headquarters for 18 wing.

The people of this area, went out of their way to make the Polish airmen welcome – they were so far from their homeland

and many, of course, had had no word from loved ones for a considerable time. All the airmen at Chailey soon became very popular with the local residents, but although my friends and I, at Fletching, never actually visited the airfield whilst it was operational, we knew people who had visited there, and thus, through conversations, we got to know something of the procedures there – nothing 'secret' though – and we always bore in mind that – 'Careless talk cost lives!'

Whilst the Spitfires were operational, we were aware of their comings and goings and, from time to time, we would stand in the recreation ground and look towards the South Downs and, mainly on clear days, the aircraft were visible as they took off or came in to land, after returning from a mission. Having this operational airfield so close to us, gave us an added feeling of protection.

During 1944 the airfield was to become one of the most important ones, playing host to the controlling sector for nine squadrons in three wings – which were based at Coolham and Selsey as well as Chailey. These three wings were eventually to provide low cover to the invading forces on D-Day, whilst they were establishing the beach heads.

By the beginning of May we had heard that, from Moscow, Marshal Stalin had 'instructed' Bulgaria, Hungary and Rumania to wage war on Germany, and in London, Anthony Eden had spoken about General Franco agreeing to reduce Spanish links with Germany. Because of pieces of news such as these, it was felt that the invasion of German occupied France, was now, definitely imminent.

At that time, although everything to do with the forthcoming D. Day was supposed to be 'Top Secret'- Sussex had become a 'beehive' of activity, with army manoeuvres and movements going on all over the place, and it, more or less, went without saying that the invasion – 'could be any day soon.' The southern counties, including Sussex, soon became 'Top Security Zones' – with passes required for journeys outside your own area – and your journeys really did have to be necessary! It seemed that there were army vehicles everywhere, including tanks and bren-gun carriers, and dispatch riders could be seen 'whizzing about' all over the place – obviously delivering messages of some importance!

Back at home, I remember father telling us that thousands of troops were coming into the area and living under canvas in various camps and that these areas were strictly off limits to civilians – with all or most of the soldiers being confined to their camps. "This must be the invasion coming up!" I remember father saying.

The weather, at this time, also seemed to be ideal for crossing the channel. Towards the end of May there were some beautiful summer days, with well above average temperatures for the time of the year – on May 29th a temperature of 91 degrees Fahrenheit, a record for May, was recorded at Horsham. I remember that, at school, we were all dressed in our 'height of summer clothes' and all the windows were left wide open – as they were at home. I also remember that the 'atmosphere' amongst the Canadian troops seemed to be different, and many of those that we approached in our quest for Sweet Caporal cards, whilst still being pleasant to us, none the less, seemed preoccupied and always in a hurry.

In the early stages of the war, sign posts had been removed in case of invasion – a slowing up method, making it difficult for strangers to find where they were. Now, the security was tightened even further and adverts appeared on billboards reminding people that 'careless talk costs lives.' One particular message to the people, which appeared in the papers and on posters said – 'SH – SH – H – H – Now more than ever, careless talk costs lives. The Germans are desperate for any scrap of information about invasion plans. BE CAREFUL!'

We children soon found that places such as Sheffield Park and Searles were now tightly guarded, making our visits to them – for a time – just about impossible.

In early June, the weather changed and it became somewhat unsettled with some rain and low flying cloud. On Monday June 5th we were ignorant of the fact that, because of inclement weather, a huge 'armada' that had been set to sail from the shores of southern England that day, had had to stay where it was – but the next day was to be different.

In the early morning of the sixth of June, it was immediately noticeable to us that the whole area seemed quieter than usual – there seemed to be no troops about at all! This 'eerie' quiet was quickly shattered by the sounds of hundreds of aircraft flying overhead, in the direction of the channel. I remember I got up much earlier than usual that morning – as did many of my friends, and we quickly cycled to a viewpoint just outside the village, in time to see aircraft

towing gliders on their way towards the channel and France –
the invasion had begun!

The aeroplanes seemed to be passing overhead 'forever' –
like a swarm of giant bees! It seemed that every type of aircraft
that could tow a glider, was doing so. There were Stirlings,
Dakotas, Halifaxes and many others as well – it seemed a
wonder that they didn't collide.

We were to learn afterwards that when the exodus of
troops, from areas such as Sheffield Park, had taken place
the night before – leaving the area devoid of troops, apart
from 'skeleton staffs' – there were several accidents from
this huge force of tanks, lorries and guns passing through
the previously quiet and narrow country roads.

The local vicarage wall was demolished and the repairs
later done to it can still be seen to this day. Sadly, a crew
member of one of the tanks, fell off and was run over by the
following vehicle – there was a service in the church for him,
before his body was taken to the Canadian cemetery at
Brookwood, in Surrey.

At home, on the radio, we soon started getting reports
about the invasion on the beaches of Normandy. Later in
the day, the Brighton Evening Argus headlined –
'MIGHTY AIR, LAND AND SEA ATTACK,' and went
on to say that tanks and other vehicles had been landed as
well as troops.

In Sussex, we were later to learn of some of the huge
amount of work that had gone on in preparation for the
invasion – some of it right under our noses, without our
realising what was going on. Apart from Sheffield Park and

Searles and all the troops that we had seen under canvas in various camps, a lot of the highly secret preparation, had taken place in nearby areas – particularly in the Newhaven area. Apparently, at Piddinghoe – not far from Newhaven and situated just near a tidal stretch of the Ouse – a secret project had gone ahead so that it was possible to conceal a large amount of invasion craft from being seen by German reconnaissance planes. A canal had been dug to by-pass a bend in the river, and this had been disguised with various types of foliage, and also, large quantities of camouflaged netting. The ships in the harbour, getting ready for the invasion, were also shrouded in this netting.

After this part of the invasion force had left Newhaven Harbour, this area in Sussex was still very much involved in the invasion, in as much that a nerve centre, which was to co-ordinate a large part of the invasion fleet, had been installed in a network of tunnels and rooms below the village of South Heighton – just near Newhaven. From these corridors and rooms, many of the planners and strategists were able to keep in constant contact with what was going on, in a line from Dover to Portsmouth. This was also to see that ships from different embarking ports met at assembly points in the channel correctly – before moving on towards off-shore areas near the Normandy beaches. These tunnels had been excavated and built in 1941 as an essential part of a Naval shore base, in what looked to be a port which would soon play a significant part in the war, because of its important position on the south coast and nearness to the French coast. The base was called H.M.S. Forward.

During the next few days, we heard mainly encouraging bits of news about the allied advances into Normandy and these reports led to many people thinking that peace could be just around the corner and that, in any case, the Germans would be so busy fighting rearguard actions in their retreat, that we at home would be left in peace at last. This assumption proved to be incorrect, because on June 13th 1944 – a week after D-Day – the Germans unleashed a new and terrifying weapon on the south east of England. It was the day that the enemy sent over the first of their unmanned aircraft – the VI Rocket – or 'Doodlebug,' as it quickly and 'unaffectionately' became known as!

The first of these 'flying bombs' came down on the village of Swanscombe in Kent, the second one though, came to earth at the village of Cuckfield in Sussex – not all that far from us. These missiles were aimed at London, but many of them came down in other areas in the south east corner, causing damage and devastation wherever they exploded – which is to say nothing of the terror installed in us when we heard the deep growling roar of their engines. This was an unmistakable sound, which would suddenly cut out – then silence – then the explosion. According to the records, of the ten 'Doodlebugs' that were sent over the channel that day, just four managed to find land.

By the end of June, nearly 2000 of these devastating weapons had been sent across the channel and this had set a big problem for the air force and those on the ground manning the guns, who were trying to shoot them down before they could do much damage, with loss of life. The VI flew at a height of between 2000 and 3000 feet, and this made it difficult for the gunners, because it was too high for the light guns and too low for the heavy ones. It was decided that by using new kinds of shells and positioning many more guns in a line from near Newhaven to just beyond Dover, that this would give the guns the effective range that they required. It would also give unrestricted field of fire at the VI's coming in from the channel – with the shells and destroyed VI's falling harmlessly into the sea. This would also give the RAF a better go at them as they flew from the coast to the north downs – where they would run into more defences in the shape of large numbers of barrage balloons.

The pilots of our fighter planes soon discovered that it was hazardous to shoot down one of these 'flying bombs' if they were too close to it; the safe distance was about 200 yards – certainly no less! Some pilots, if they were out of ammunition, would fly close to the VI and place one of the fighter's wings against one of the missile's wings, and 'tip' it over – always bearing in mind where it was likely to land.

On 9th September, we got news of another type of flying bomb – the V2 – which was even more devastating than the Doodlebug. The first of these had exploded in England the day before, but thankfully we never saw or heard any of these at Fletching. This, of course, was terrifying for those who were in the range of these deadly missiles, which could demolish a whole street. Fortunately, both these and the VI's were soon to come to an end, with the destruction of the launching sites by the advancing allied troops.

135

As I have said, at Fletching we never actually sighted any of the V2's, but we did see plenty of Doodlebugs passing overhead on their deadly missions – I shall never forget the horrible and unmistakable sound they made. Recently, at an exhibition to do with World War II, I heard a recording of the actual noise of a Doodlebug, and when it came to the part where the engine suddenly stopped, it seemed that the hairs on the back of my neck stood up – the attacks were so terrifying that my memory cells had immediately been alerted to danger. In those days we knew that if the engine cut out, and it was overhead, we had to find immediate cover and hope for the best – fortunately, for us, none did!

By 6th December, after consistent and heavy bombing by the allies, it was reported that 20 million Germans were homeless and, by the Christmas of 1944, it was thought that the end of the war was very close.

On April 30th 1945 it was announced that Hitler was dead, and on Tuesday 8th May, Mr. Churchill, on the radio, told the nation that hostilities in Europe would officially end at one minute past midnight that night – the war in Europe was over!

May 8th 1945, will stay in my memory for the rest of my life, it wasn't only the end of the war in Europe, it was also the day before my fourteenth birthday. We went to school as usual on that day, but after the whole school was assembled we walked over to the church for a special thanksgiving service; after which we were given the rest of the day off – a special holiday – a celebration day.

My grandmother had been saving some pre-war fireworks for this occasion and I was given them to let off that night – a night that was celebrated by the whole of the country, with firework displays, dancing in the streets, parties going on everywhere and all the pubs filled to overflowing. One thing that I particularly remember of that time, was not having to cover the windows – there was no more blackout. It seemed odd, but 'warming' to see the lights showing from every house in the village.

At home, we had many visitors that night, and mother opened some bottles of her wine to celebrate with – quite potent stuff from long maturity. There weren't many amongst the adults who visited us, who, when they went home later on, went on their way anything less than 'a little tipsy' – it was a happy night, one full of joy, when many a cup must have run over, in what became one gigantic party for the whole of the nation.

Although the war in the far east was still raging, we at home now faced the first days and months of peace, and although there was still food rationing and a massive job to be done in putting the country back in shape, we faced this task with relish and enthusiasm. This was a new dawn and the ways of life we had known for so long were soon to change – sometimes dramatically.

Chapter Eight

Peace At Last – Working For A Living

T he first big happening during the new won peace – something which was quite a shock to many people – was the defeat of Mr. Churchill's Conservative government by the Labour Party in the general election. To many it seemed that Mr. Churchill, who had guided us so successfully through the war years, instead of receiving the country's eternal gratitude – had now been 'kicked in the teeth.' However, we weren't at war any more and the majority of people didn't want things to return to the pre-war ways of government and the new labour policy was what appealed the most to the voters now. The election took place on July 26th 1945 and, after a day of heavy balloting, Clement Attlee was elected to lead the labour government – a government that would last until 1951.

At home, in the country at Fletching, I had now started taking on part time jobs to earn a few shillings each week; I wanted to add this extra money to the pocket money I had been saving towards buying a brand new bicycle. Over the years, all the bicycles I had owned had been bought second hand – my parents had bought my first one for me for the grand sum of seven shillings – this bicycle had had quite a few owners in the village, it even became known as the village bike; it was for 'beginners' and it always changed hands for the same price.

I left Fletching School at the age of fourteen, at the end of the summer term of 1945 and, although I had failed the equivalent of what is now the eleven plus, I none the less sat the entrance examination to go to the technical college at Lewes – and just scraped through! So, in September of that year, I was due to start a two year course in building construction.

My ambitions at this time were prone to change as the months went past, but one thing I particularly remember was that my father was adamant that he didn't want me to work at the saw mill – which was just as well, as I didn't want to either!

I had a Saturday job at the baker's shop – from 8 am to mid-day and earned the princely sum of two shillings and sixpence for those four hours. My jobs at the baker's included chopping up sticks to keep the fires going for the baking, helping to take the newly baked bread out of the baking tins and placing the loaves on racks to cool off – a good job in the winter, but too hot in the summer – and, after this, I would deliver loaves locally, carrying the bread and rolls in a basket that seemed to be as big as myself. After a while, I started work even earlier on a Saturday – so that I could take on a butcher's round as well. To do this job, I had to ride a 'monster' delivery bicycle, which was too big for me to ride in the conventional manner, so I had to ride it with one leg through the frame, between the cross bar and the down tube – not very comfortable or safe, but it worked for most of the time and I got the job done. There was one time however, when the brakes failed and, after 'sailing' over the handlebars, I went straight into a ditch – shooting most of the meat into the ditch with me.

Eventually, the day arrived when I had saved enough money for my new bicycle – a special and exciting day for me. I caught the bus to Uckfield clutching my hard earned savings tightly and protectively in my hand. In those days there was a shortage of materials to build the bicycles, so I had had to join a waiting list. At last, after a long wait, my turn had come and, on arriving at the shop, I immediately saw the bicycle that I wanted in the window; it's difficult to describe my feelings at that moment – just sheer joy, I suppose! The bicycle cost £18.18.0. – eighteen guineas, in other words – and, after I had counted out every note and coin, I found that I had just enough over to buy a saddle bag.

I could only just reach the pedals, even with the saddle at its lowest position, but this didn't deter me from riding it home – eagerly changing gear at every opportunity; in those days, just three gears were considered a luxury. I remember, I could hardly wait for it to get dark that night, so that I could try out the Dynohub lighting.

From then on, this bicycle took me further afield than I had ever biked before on any of my second hand bikes. One of the first places I went to was Barcombe Mills, to fish in the river Ouse near the big millpool and other stretches of the river near there. We used to fish for sea trout, which came up the river from the sea at Newhaven to spawn in the quieter stretches. Unfortunately, we never caught one of these highly sought after fish, but, none the less, had many memorable fishing outings on the stretch of the river from the mill to Brown's Boathouse. I remember that there used to be monkeys in the trees, kept as pets, near this remarkable boathouse, where they let out flat bottomed canoes so that one could explore the non tidal stretches of the river and its small tributaries.

Having a good and reliable bike now, also made it possible for me to go to the pictures in Uckfield more frequently – leaving the bike with friends of the family, who lived in Uckfield, whilst I was in the cinema.

In September, when I started at the technical college, I cycled to Sheffield Park station, where I left the bicycle each day for a small monthly fee, and then caught the train to Lewes. This train came from East Grinstead, on its journey through West Hoathly, Horsted Keynes, Sheffield Park, Newick, Barcombe and then Lewes. I had to leave home at 7.15 each morning, and soon got to know others, who were making the same journey and also going to the technical college. These journeys could be quite hazardous – not because of the way the train was driven, but because of what we got up to on the journeys to and fro. We would, quite frequently, open train doors whilst hurtling through the countryside, and we often had 'water bomb' fights with other pupils standing on the platforms of the stations we went through – not caring much about the fact that we obviously had the advantage, being on the train! On looking back on some of those journeys, I feel it's a wonder that we all survived without any serious injuries.

Back at home, with the rationing continuing, our diet was much the same as it had been during the war years and, although mother was still making her annual supply of homemade wine, the quantity of bottles made was small in comparison to the pre war years, when you could buy as much sugar as you liked – it would be several more years before things got back to normal again.

After spending two years at technical college, I was accepted as a junior draughtsman in a job that entailed tracing maps for the War Agriculture Committee in Lewes, and spent the next three years at this job.

In agriculture during the war years, many areas on the downs had been cultivated to grow extra crops – food being so scarce, farmers had to use every inch of land available and cereals and vegetables, in particular, were in big demand. There were also quite a few new crops grown in the area – such as flax and sugar beet. More and more tractors came onto the scene and the days of horse drawn carts and wagons were soon phased out. This was also, unfortunately, the time when it started to become quite a rare sight to see the ploughs being pulled by horses and guided by the ploughman.

During the war years and for a while afterwards, we often saw land girls out working on the fields and, in the evenings, coming into the village for the occasional quiet drink or when dances were held in the village hall.

There were also prisoners of war working on the land until well after the war had ended – both Germans and Italians. I remember people saying that the Italians were mainly 'workshy' and seemed to spend most of their time lazing around, singing songs and trying to flirt with the land girls – if they happened to be working alongside them. They could easily be recognised, not only by their Latin looks, but also by the patches that were sewn on the uniform jackets and trousers. The German POW's mainly worked well though; they were thorough and keen to make a good job of whatever they put their hands to – Teutonic thoroughness, I suppose! Many of these prisoners were still here in 1947 – some of them, up to 1948 – but eventually they were sent home to get on with their lives in the new found peace in Europe. For the Germans, there was a country still in devastation, which would take much putting together again after all the bombings and general waging of war.

Also during the war, when the flax was ready, some of us children were given time off from school to help with it's harvesting. A swathe had to be cleared round the edge of the field by hand before the harvesting machine could be used – we were paid for this, as well as for picking up potatoes in the autumn.

Many of the farmers carried on using the extra acreage they had been asked to take on during the war years and they were soon looking for permanent farm workers to replace the POW's and women from the Land Army. Whilst the thought had briefly passed through my mind – whether my vocation in life lay in this direction, I never seriously entertained the idea – my ambitions were for a very different way of life. None the less, being a born and bred 'country

143

boy,' I have always taken a keen interest in the land – especially the farms close to the Fletching and Piltdown areas.

One farm that was a bit different to the other farms in the area, was called Moon's Farm – apart from the usual crops and cattle you would see on Sussex farms, they also grew hops. I feel that I should put in this book something of the workings of a Sussex farm in those days and I have chosen this farm and one other one because of letters received about their workings. The first one is from John Pye, the son of Laurence Pye, who owned Moon's farm for a number of years – the letter tells, in interesting detail, how the farm was worked and includes a piece about the hops. He writes:

'As I remember it, it was in 1943 that my father, Laurence Pye bought Moon's from Jack Kennard. My father had had several thousand acres of land on farms on the downs on the outskirts of Brighton, but the army had taken over most of this land for training purposes.

There were about two hundred acres at Moon's Farm in those days, comprising cereals, grass and eleven acres of hops. We also reared cattle and this included a house cow. There was a staff of four, who lived in tied cottages on the farm. A tributary of the river Ouse formed one boundary of the farm – at one spot, a weir had been built and this provided a lovely, though cold, swimming pool.

The hop gardens were the most westerly in the south east of England. Each spring the poles were put up and the stringing followed this. During the growing season there

144

were several sprayings or washing of the hops – necessary to keep diseases at bay. The fertility of the ground was largely supplied by 'shoddy' – wool like waste which came from the north country in big bales.

Hop picking always started around the 21st September – a little later than in Kent, where, before the war, my father had farmed many acres of hops. The pickers, mostly all being local, made their own way to come and pick – although we did collect some from Maresfield and other villages. Payment was per bushel picked – the measurer scooped them out of the bins they picked into and emptied them into 'pokes' – loosely woven hessian sacks. These were then taken by tractor and trailer (in earlier days by horse and cart, of course) to the Oast House, where there were two kilns for drying the hops. The upper floor, where the hops were spread out to dry, had a hessian covered floor and, after they had been levelled out, the fires downstairs were lit. Welsh Anthracite was the only fuel used, but sulphur was added to this – this would give the dried hops a more healthy, brighter looking lustre and would help increase the price we got at the time of selling to the agents, acting on behalf of the brewers.

Our crop was taken to Newick station and dispatched by rail to the factors in London.

As far as the cereals were concerned, we harvested with a binder and stacked the corn in a stackyard, to await threshing in the winter. This was done by a local contractor who used a traction engine. I well remember one particular day when he arrived to 'light up,' but, as he was late and to speed up the

145

process, he 'shot' what he thought was paraffin into the fire box – it was petrol – thankfully he wasn't too seriously burnt, but definitely 'well singed!'

I remember that our tractor driver was a very useful man to have around the farm, a dab hand at DIY, he would say, if something needed repairing – "I can soon 'fornicate' something for that!"

The second letter about farming in those bygone days, came from Henry Robinson, he says:

'My father had a small farm on the Chailey/Newick border – it was all grass and used for calf rearing. In the winter of 1938/39 I was sent, as a pupil, to Mr. John Martin at Netherall Farm, at Fletching. Mr. Martin was a very good farmer, on traditional lines – some of his family are still around. He kept a hand-milked herd of black and white cows and grew wheat, oats, turnips and marrow stemmed kale – he also kept a flock of sheep.

His method of growing wheat is a good example of arable farming of that area in those days. Firstly, he mixed his seed corn with tar and hot water, on a barn floor – this was to keep the rooks off it! After this it was dusted with slaked lime, to make it sowable. A field, which had probably grown turnips grazed off by sheep, would be ploughed by two horses – at the rate of one acre a day. It was then sown and broadcast on the furrow by hand by Mr. Martin – it was then harrowed in straight away. When the field was completed, a single horse drew water furrows where needed, to draw off surface water and from then, until the corn was up, no-one was allowed to walk on the field for fear of leaving footmarks, which might hold water. It was a wet farm and Mr. Martin was very particular.

In the winter, the sheep were folded on turnips and one of my jobs was to help the shepherd pitch the folds a day ahead – so the sheep had fresh keep every day. In those days general labour was cheap and plentiful and I think that the wage for a general farm worker was about 34/6d for a long week.'

My wages, in my job in Lewes, were 35/- a week, but from this I had to pay for my keep at home and my fares to work – so there wasn't much left over. I was quite happy in the company of my friends, with whom – on my new bicycle, which was constantly in use – we explored much of the Sussex countryside.

In later years, to supplement my wages slightly and also for a bit of good walking exercise, I would go beating for the shoots on Searles Estate – it wasn't much pay but it was out in the fresh air and we used to go through some beautiful countryside. I would go in the company of a friend of mine, John Fountain, the son of the gamekeeper at Searles. Mr. Fountain would keep control of the line of beaters by a series of blasts on his whistle – it was important to keep in line as accidents could happen. Beating the woods was alright whatever the weather, but there was nothing worse than driving game, on a wet winter morning, through a field of waist high, wet, cold kale – one would be wet for the rest of the beat. We had our lunch at the keepers lodge and provided our own food, but the liquid refreshments – bottles of beer were provided by the shoot.

147

After lunch we would continue beating for several more 'drives' – then return to the lodge to get paid and perhaps be given a rabbit from the 'bag.' Lads under sixteen years of age would get 5/- for their days work; those from sixteen to eighteen would get 10/- and the men, £1 – which you could buy quite a bit with in those days.

Although there were friendships with girls in those days, there weren't many really serious romances. From time to time, small groups of us, of both sexes, armed with just a few shillings extra in our pockets, would go by train to Brighton for a day out. In those days, for a 'country boy,' this was something of a major event. On the journey to Lewes, the line was single track for quite a distance, so a special staff, like a huge key (carried by the engine driver) would be fitted into a device that would stop another train from entering the single track at the same time – this had to be handed in at the end of the single track by the engine driver leaning out of the cab – the reverse had to carried out, of course, on the return journey. This single track ran from Sheffield Park to Culver Junction, where the Uckfield line joined the track – a distance of about nine miles.

I remember I was always enthralled by the view as we went over the big viaduct as we approached Brighton station – there were more houses than I had ever seen before. I was fascinated by my first walk down Queens Road and West Street, and made a mental note to visit the ice rink there some time. (Now, sadly, gone.) After this, we went on to one of the beaches, which during the war, had been barbed wired off from the public – with many of them mined

148

against possible invasion. We went on both the Palace Pier and the West Pier on most of these outings and, I remember, I particularly enjoyed playing on the penny machines, spending some of my pocket money on 'The Laughing Policman,' or 'The Haunted House' or, more daringly, 'What the Butler saw!'

We often used to eat our sandwiches on the beach – I remember on one occasion getting too close to the water on a day that the sea was rough, and getting soaked by an extra large wave, which crashed with huge force on the shingle just in front of me.

Back at home, life carried on in much the same fashion, but these were changing times, with many of the old ways making way for new ideas and new ideals.

In the aftermath of the war, there were still a few deserters from the forces roaming the countryside – just a step or so in front of the law – before the time of any amnesty. It was thought that a few of these might have joined the tramps which frequented a section of road near to Fletching, which was called Tramps Alley – so called because the woods on either side of the road, especially during the winter months, were often the sheltering place or temporary home for tramps or 'gentlemen of the road' – as they were sometimes called. These woods were particularly favoured by the tramps because there was a stream there which was quite fast running and didn't freeze over during the coldest of the winter weather – there was also a good supply of firewood. During the war years no fires could be lit because of the blackout, so it must have been difficult for them to cook at nights. However, to keep warm and protected from the elements, they used to construct rough shelters, which they used to call 'Benders.' These shelters would be made by bending living Hazel trees and covering them with tarpaulin sheets, which were usually obtained from local farmers – by one means or another!

Poaching, of course, was rife and many a pheasant, hare or rabbit found its way into the communal cooking pot. Throughout the years, there were quite frequent cases, reported in the papers, of these men being fined for obtaining there livelihood off the 'fat of the land.' The laws concerning these ways of life were soon to become even more vigilant, until eventually, their visits to the wood became mainly – just a memory.

Nearer to home, but on the same road as this, there is a small steepish incline called, Haunted Oak Hill – so named after an unfortunate individual committed suicide by hanging himself from an oak tree there, in the latter part of the last century. I remember that, as a child, I wouldn't go along this section of the road after dark – several of the locals had sworn that they had seen the ghost of this person, still hanging from the tree, probably just after coming home from the pub, or perhaps, after just a bit too much home made wine!

On the opposite side of the road to this wood was a 'shaw' or small wood, where, as a family we would pick primroses and bluebells – this was when I was very young, but I can remember going there in later years to pick hazel nuts in the autumn. There was also a giant beech tree here, on which many of our group and plenty of other children had carved their name or initials, on its trunk or lower branches.

Whilst I was attending Fletching school, I was always very keen on sport – especially football and cricket and, after leaving school, in the years before joining up, I often played cricket for the village team and have memories of many enjoyable games played during that time. I carried on playing for the team after I was demobbed and can particularly remember playing against comedian Jimmy Edward's 'Handlebar' Club team – this was in the early 1950's – but, I feel I should include it here; Jimmy and his brother Alan had come to live and farm at Atherall's Farm in the village, at about that time. The Handlebar Club was made up of members, all of whom 'sported' superb, 'lengthy,' magnificently shaped mustachio's – 'Handlebars' – as they called them. We played against these gentlemen on several occasions – it was always great fun.

Amongst other traditions that carried on after the war, were the May Day celebrations. The main events for these would take place on the recreation ground, and consisted of dancing round the maypole by the younger children as well as country dancing by the older girls and sword dancing by the more mature boys. The maypole dancing was a very old custom and still survives to this day in quite a few parts of the country. Many hours of practice were necessary before the complicated plaiting of the coloured ribbons looked to be in any sort of order – there would be much frustration and many tears when some unfortunate child went 'over' instead of 'under' the next ribbon. The 'worst' thing to

151

happen to a small boy of seven or eight years of age, was to have to hold hands with a girl – even worse though, was having to put his arm around her waist – there would be much teasing afterwards. The music was provided by a wind-up gramophone (later, cassette player) – woe betide the child in charge of the gramophone, if they let it run down whilst the dance was in progress.

The swords used in the sword dancing were only made of wooden laths, so there was no chance of any of the participants getting cut – although it wasn't unknown for some of the dancers to exact revenge, for some reason, by means of a sly whack or tripping up with the 'sword.' When performed properly, the sword dance was a skilful and elegant thing to behold – I progressed from the maypole to the sword dance and, if I am honest, it was enjoyable to take part in.

The country dancing also has its roots back in time – possibly as far back as the maypole dancing or perhaps even longer ago than that – the dancing was performed by the older girls and was usually led by the May Queen. The May Queen would also travel round the village in a decorated horse drawn wagon, pulled by a pair of cart horses – also decorated. She would be accompanied by her attendants, who would also be wearing long dresses and garlands of spring flowers in their hair. Two small boys would act as page boys to carry the May Queen's train and, on reaching the recreation ground, the May Queen would be crowned by her predecessor and the dancing would begin. One of the perks of celebrating May Day in this manner, was that the

May Queen would ask for a days holiday to be granted to all the children; this was always given to the rousing call for – 'Three cheers for the May Queen!'

In May 1949, my call-up papers arrived and later in that month I had to go to Brighton for a medical. In September, I travelled to Padgate to begin eighteen months national service – this was put up to two years shortly after I joined up, but, none the less, I enjoyed all of it.

As I left home on that final morning, on my way to Padgate, I reflected on the different milestones of my life and the memories came flooding back. I had been lucky enough to be born in a loving family, in a beautiful area – something I had taken full advantage of over the years. Also, I had grown up during an amazing time in History, the likes of which are never likely to be seen again. Most importantly, I remember the lasting friendships that had developed between people in the area, at a time when the country had had its back to the wall and when we were all in the same 'boat' together. Although we suffered many hardships, we also seemed to gain in stature as people and this, of course, has enhanced the memories to be golden and unforgettable.

Epilogue

I n putting together my memories of the formative years of my life – which span some significant times in the history of this country – apart from wanting my friends and future generations of my family to know what it was like growing up during that period of time, I have also, with assistance from Sussex author David J. Knowles, put together a record of some of the history and ways of life through the ages, which I hope will be both interesting as well as enlightening to any future readers.

I know of quite a few villages and communities where, recently, people have been encouraged to put down their memories of ways of life and happenings during their lifetimes in this amazingly progressive century. It is a pity that such records weren't commonly kept in the centuries gone by, but at least, by writing of one's memories now, there should be good records of this unique period in history left for future generations to browse over, absorb and learn from – something of a far cry from the dark ages or even the last century, of which, so little is known about the lives of the 'ordinary' people, as individuals.

Apart from while I was serving the two years of my national service in the RAF, I have lived in Sussex for the whole of my life. During those years of national service, I thought of making the RAF my career – but this wasn't to be. After I was demobbed I came back to Fletching and carried on living with my parents – that was in September 1951. I didn't carry on with the job in Lewes, but instead took on jobs in the building industry where the money was better – thus enabling me to afford my hobbies. Eventually, I worked for the road safety section of East Sussex County Council until retiring in 1996, after working there for twenty seven and a half years.

In my free time I carried on in very much the same manner as I had done before joining up. I joined Isfield Angling Club and spent many hours fishing the river Ouse again – especially at Barcombe Mills; I also played a lot more cricket for the village team. However, it was at this time that my interest in motor cycles became my main hobby. I passed my driving test within a month of starting to ride and during the time I rode these fascinating machines, I owned forty different motor cycles in as many years. It was through riding one of them that I first met my wife, Rosemary. She was working as a kennel maid in kennels just opposite Isfield station; I was visiting a friend there – also a keen motor cyclist. Rosemary had been born at Burwash, in Sussex, but her parents had moved to Isfield to work on a small estate there. We were married at Isfield Parish Church on Christmas Eve 1955. Our son Gavin was born in Crowborough in 1963 and our daughter Jo, in Eastbourne in 1960 – so we are all

Sussex born and bred, including our three grandchildren, (Jo's children) Zoe, Hannah and Jack.

From time to time, I meet my old friend, Tony Welfare, and when we meet we always go over the old days together – conversations which usually include the words "Do you remember 'such and such' a thing happening – or "I saw so and so recently." Sadly, our good friend Frank Kingsland passed away several years ago – we shared many an adventure alongside him and he often comes into our reminiscences.

In Piltdown, the pond and the common are as beautiful as ever and Fletching still retains its beauty and character; unfortunately, all the shops, except the thriving butcher's shop, have closed down, but both the pubs, The Griffin and The Rose And Crown are still going strong – only Granddad Butcher, the village molecatcher, is missing from his seat by the fireplace at The Rose And Crown. Searles House had been so badly looked after, that it eventually had to be pulled down – it is difficult to imagine now that there was ever a house there. The view of Searles was one of my family's favourite sights when out on a Sunday 'constitutional.'

My father, Thomas Ellis Butcher, died in 1975 and my mother, Winifred Elsie, passed away two years later, in 1977. Many of my relatives – going back over a long span of years – now rest in the peace and serenity of Fletching churchyard.

Amongst the many hobbies I have taken up over the years are photography and golf. I was a member of Seaford Head

Golf Club for quite some time, but, about ten years ago, I was diagnosed as having Parkinson's Disease and as a result of this I have, regrettably, had to pack up playing.

My wife and I now live at Newhaven, and have done for the past thirty one years. This Sussex port is where the Ouse comes down to the sea – so, I was born just near where this river of character still enjoys its early life and I expect to spend the rest of my days here, where, in its full maturity, the river joins the sea – a constant cycle – rich in life.

Michael Butcher with his wife Rosemary at an annual meeting of RAF Lichfield Association.

Michael often visits Fletching and other places that became so familiar to him in the earlier days of his life.

He is photographic secretary of R.A.F. Lichfield Association which meets on the first Friday in September each year. This is followed the day afterwards with a service in Lichfield Cathedral.

For the past ten years Michael has suffered from Parkinson's Disease and is now chairman of the Eastbourne Parkinson's Society.

As a hobby, Michael enjoys attending The Creative Writing Centre in Newhaven. Michael and Rosemary have lived in this pleasant Sussex port for the past thirty one years.